WHY CAN'T WE GET ANYTHING DONE AROUND HERE?

WHY CAN'T WE GET ANYTHING DONE AROUND HERE?

The Smart Manager's Guide to Executing the Work That Delivers Results

Robert E. Lefton, Ph.D.
Jerome T. Loeb

McGraw-Hill

NEW YORK CHICAGO SAN FRANCISCO LISBON
LONDON MADRID MEXICO CITY MILAN NEW DELHI
SAN JUAN SEOUL SINGAPORE SYDNEY TORONTO

The McGraw-Hill Companies

6 7 8 9 10 DOH/DOH 15 14 13

ISBN 0-07-143006-7

This publication is designed to provide accurate and authoritative information in regard to the subject matter covered. It is sold with the understanding that the publisher is not engaged in rendering legal, accounting, or other professional service. If legal advice or other expert assistance is required, the services of a competent professional person should be sought.

—From a declaration of principles jointly adopted by a committee of the American Bar Association and a committee of publishers.

McGraw-Hill books are available at special quantity discounts to use as premiums and sales promotions, or for use in corporate training programs. For more information, please write to the Director of Special Sales, Professional Publishing, McGraw-Hill, Two Penn Plaza, New York, NY 10121-2298. Or contact your local bookstore.

This book is printed on recycled, acid-free paper containing a minimum of 50% recycled, de-inked fiber.

Library of Congress Cataloging-in-Publication Data

Lefton, Robert Eugene.
Why can't we get anything done around here? : the smart manager's guide to executing the work that delivers results / by Robert E. Lefton and Jerome T. Loeb.
p. cm.
ISBN 0-07-143006-7 (alk. paper)
1. Management. I. Loeb, Jerome T. II. Title.
HD31.L3734 2004
658—dc22

2003019526

I dedicate this book to my entire family—my wife, my children and their partners, and my grandchildren. They are very important in my life and I love loving them. I hope that over the years I keep developing the skills of doing so. It is a gold star activity.

—Robert E. Lefton, Ph.D.

I dedicate this book to my wonderful teachers. I have kept a mental list of the special teachers who have helped me in so many ways. These include my parents, brother, wife, and children; other relatives; friends and acquaintances; teachers in school; and business associates. I particularly want to thank a teacher, the late Fred Werremeyer, who taught me to teach, and a business associate, Dave Farrell, who taught me to stretch.

—Jerome T. Loeb

CONTENTS

FOREWORD

Andrall E. Pearson

Improving productivity is a high-priority challenge for every executive, especially in today's increasingly competitive environment. Many books on this subject are too generic to be useful, or they are written from too lofty a perspective (the view from 30,000 feet).

This book has been written by two gifted practitioners—one an outstanding business executive, the other a top-notch human relations expert. Their core idea is simple: Most unproductive work in any organization stems from poor decisions about who should be assigned to do the task in the first place. The authors provide a simple and practical tool that any manager can use to make effective work assignment decisions. And they back it up with live examples of good and bad decisions and practices.

The authors describe a totally different approach to thinking about the way to get work done effectively and how to identify and root out unproductive work.

As one who has been deeply involved in business management for over 50 years, I learned about a technique that could have saved me considerable anguish and made me a more effective decision maker and allocator of work. Therefore, I heartily recommend *Why Can't We Get Anything Done Around Here?* to executives and managers at any level.

INTRODUCTION

This book is the result of a collaboration of a business executive trying to help an organization get more done and a psychologist with extensive experience helping organizations with human resources issues.

In his positions as president and, later, chairman of the board of the May Department Stores Company, Jerome Loeb was responsible for the nonmerchandising functions of the company. In this capacity he spent a considerable amount of time at the company's divisions, meeting with many of the division executives to learn firsthand "what was going on." This included communicating ideas from other divisions, helping with priorities and problems, and assessing organizational needs.

These meetings generally were rewarding and productive, and the organization was talented and motivated (this being a period when May increased earnings per share for 27 consecutive years). However, there was often a frustration that went with trying to complete the unrelenting amount of work that faced the organization. This went beyond the usual tradeoffs about priorities. People were working hard—very hard—but without getting a commensurate amount of things *done*.

Mr. Loeb had many conversations about this subject with Dr. Robert Lefton, co-CEO of Psychological Associates. From their talks a model emerged that is the basis for this book. The *task management model* adds a dimension to assigning work that considers the match between the task and the person assigned to do it. The model also identifies possible errors. When applied, the model makes it easier to understand and then to avoid many of these errors.

Of course, no simple model can cover the many considerations that go into the assignment of tasks, and this one conflicts with conventional thinking (delegate as much as possible). However, the task management model has been introduced to many executives and organizations, and reception has been enthusiastic. Those who use it find it genuinely helpful. Its applicability goes beyond the assignment of tasks. It helps executives evaluate how they spend their own time.

Dr. Lefton and Mr. Loeb thank the May Company, especially David Farrell, May's CEO during much of Mr. Loeb's tenure. Dr. Lefton has enjoyed a wonderful relationship with the company and appreciates the trust conferred to him and Psychological Associates. Mr. Loeb is thankful for an enjoyable and challenging 37 years learning the business at May.

We also thank Dr. Victor R. Buzzotta, co-CEO and chairman of the board of Psychological Associates. His insights on style form the basis for Chapter 6.

Finally, thanks go to Larry Gross, without whose fine touch we could not have put our thoughts into words.

WHY CAN'T WE GET ANYTHING DONE AROUND HERE?

CHAPTER 1

ARE YOU GETTING THE RIGHT THINGS DONE?

Don't tell me how hard you work. Tell me how much you get done.

JAMES LING,
BUSINESS EXECUTIVE

It's the end of another busy day at the office. As you do every day, you have tried to practice effective management skills. You plan, you listen, you prioritize, you schedule, you delegate. You work hard to set a good example. You may even be open with people and believe in empowerment. In short, you employ a management style that is supposed to motivate people effectively.

Yet you are often frustrated and disappointed by the results. You have the nagging feeling that your efforts don't make a big enough difference where it really counts—contributing to the bottom-line performance and success of your company. More specifically, one or more of the following conveys how you feel:

- Although my people are busy at their jobs, my department's output doesn't improve much from year to year.
- I have worked on developing an enlightened management style. It is supposed to instill a "go get 'em" attitude in people. Yet, when the productivity of my department is tallied up,

somehow it's often less than the departments run by my "less enlightened" colleagues.

- Try as I might to get my people to perform when I need them, it seems that when a really important task needs to be done, I have to do it myself.
- Certain projects seem to hang around forever. Frankly, some days I wish that I could wipe the slate clean and start fresh either with different work to be done or new people.
- Although I am supposedly in charge of my direct reports, I often feel as if I am on the outside of my department looking in at a process over which I have little control.

These statements all have something in common. They all reveal an underlying impression that people are not getting the right things done. This is a valid concern. After all, "getting the right things done" is the measure of performance in an organization. In essence, it is a definition of performance itself.

GETTING BACK TO BASICS

Ironically, managers frequently do not even think of this concern as they go about dealing with the workload in front of them. While caught up in the minute-by-minute decisions they have to make all day, they may fail to step back and ask themselves some basic questions:

What tasks are people working on and why?

Are we spending more time working on the wrong tasks and less time on the ones that count?

And even if people are working on the tasks that count, do the people and the tasks match (the principal idea that we will address in Chapter 3)?

This is very simple stuff. However, not only can it be difficult to make sure that your organization has good answers to these questions, many leaders also spend days, months, and even years *not* asking them. A sort of laissez-faire attitude creeps in: "We do what we do because that's what we do, and that's how we do it!"

Nevertheless, these questions are important, and managers should be asking them all the time. Every effective high-performance leader of a department, a division, or an entire organization spends significant time making certain that he is getting the right things done.

Furthermore, this skill is not a by-product of some other desirable attributes of an effective leader. A leader doesn't get things done simply because she is good with people, charismatic, persuasive, or has an appealing personality, although these traits are real pluses for any leader. Instead, this is a fundamental characteristic of effective leaders, cultivated as a skill all its own. It is the ability (1) to size up all the things her organization *could* be doing and deciding what it *should* be doing and (2) taking the *shoulds* and getting them done!

A METHODICAL APPROACH TO RESULTS

You can learn to be a results-oriented person. This book gives you a clear and practical way to get the right things done as often as possible, one of the most important jobs you face as a manager. Specifically, it will do the following:

1. Provide you with a simple, systematic method to apply to every decision you make about what gets done and—usually overlooked—*who* does it as the key to better productivity and high performance.

Much is written today about the high level of stress and burnout in the work environment. Obviously, people are busy doing something. At the same time, when asked to respond anonymously about how they spend their time on the job, employees admit that much of what they do is "busy work," not crucial to the success of the company. Indeed, some estimate that they are achieving only 40 to 60 percent of their potential. As many as 7 of 10 employees say that they could be significantly more effective at what they do on the job. And they *want* to be more effective!

Therefore, despite the notion that today's downsized, no-nonsense workplace is supposedly stripped to the bone, people are still not being asked to perform at full capability. And this is a leadership problem. Not that managers don't try to crack the whip or offer incentives to direct reports so that they will go faster, waste less time, and take shorter breaks to accomplish more. However, our interest is in raising the percentage of work people do on the job that *actually* contributes to getting things done.

If your employees are only working at about half their potential, just imagine what it would mean if you could tap into that reserve and raise it by as little as 10 percent. If you can think logically, you can apply our systematic approach. You can focus on the tasks that are essential to your company's success and assign them to the right people.

2. Help you analyze problems that can keep managers from getting the right things done.

All of us are creatures of habit. As you will see, a lot of the unnecessary or incorrectly assigned "work" that goes on in organizations year after year is the result of unexamined assumptions and deeply ingrained habits.

This part of the book will identify and explain the mistakes that are made over and over when assigning work. Sometimes such mistakes are the result of not analyzing the situation correctly. In other cases they are the result of not thinking at all about certain important factors that should go into deciding who is right or wrong for a task. In fact, entire corporate cultures have been built on fundamentally unsound thinking about what work should be done and who should be doing it.

As you read about common problems that you can relate to your own managerial role, you will see how to apply the ideas presented here to real workplace circumstances and gain insights that you can apply immediately.

3. Show you how to go beyond managerial style and apply this effective tool for focusing on performance that will work for your personality and the particular managerial style you employ.

There is no question that cultivating an effective managerial style is essential for being a leader. However, your managerial style is not the focus of this book. While we advocate a particular leadership style that is the most effective for motivating employees, you can apply the principles presented here whatever your present style is.

4. Demonstrate how you can get your people to perform effectively, closer to the way people perform in a crisis, but without the stress and burnout associated with a crisis.

It is a common phenomenon. Organizations that appear to be busy and even overworked are often able to kick into overdrive when faced with a crisis—sometimes doubling and tripling the quality and quantity of their performance. Why is this?

When forced by a crisis to concentrate solely on important work, organizations employ many of the same principles and go through the same decision-making processes that are the basis for this book. They truly focus on getting the right things done. This successful crisis-management behavior can be applied to your organization without requiring a real crisis to make it work. You get the sizzle without going through the anguish to get the same results.

5. Explain how applying this simple tool can build a foundation for significant leadership in your organization.

Although it is simple to apply, this does not mean that this system is simple-minded. Its simplicity helps you to focus clearly and precisely on how you direct people and the work they do.

We will discuss the role you play in your organization and how you can use these methods to aim high and to realize that making good decisions about assigning work and getting the most out of the people who will do it is a signature skill of effective, high-performing leaders.

RUN FASTER BY RUNNING SMARTER

Finally, understand that while improved efficiency and productivity will result from using these techniques, this is not a book about managing your time. It's about deciding how your organization *uses* its time. It is also not concerned with installing processes to make people move faster or finding ways to squeeze more tasks into a given time frame.

Rather, increased productivity will result from putting the right people on the right tasks. Why? Because of the simple proposition that the more often people are working on something they do well, the faster it gets done—unless, of course, they despise that particular task! More about this later. Suffice it to say here that the principles you apply from reading this book get to the heart of how your people work without putting a stopwatch to what they do. You will end up running the race faster by running it smarter.

We hope you are excited about learning the many benefits of using this system. We are excited to bring it to you because it is a tested tool that was developed over many years by leaders in some of today's most dynamic and successful organizations doing business globally. It works for the smallest department. It works for the largest corporation.

So read on and discover how to hang this tool on your managerial belt, ready to use often as you go through your day making smart assignment decisions that get the right things done. Each good decision will be a building block that contributes to a structure of better productivity and higher performance.

CHAPTER 2

GOING BEYOND STYLE

Style is the hallmark of a temperament stamped upon the material at hand.

ANDRE MAUROIS,
AUTHOR

As was noted in Chapter 1, the subject of this book is not managerial style. In fact, the techniques discussed will work with virtually any style. However, because style plays an important role in managing successfully, it is important to discuss it as a context for effective task management.

Suppose that you could be transported back to the nineteenth century and dropped into the offices of some of the legendary captains of industry. You wouldn't find any books on their shelves about managerial style. It is doubtful that John D. Rockefeller, Cornelius Vanderbilt, or J. P. Morgan spent much time thinking about the interpersonal style they used in their business dealings or with their employees. Not that they didn't have plenty of style. They just didn't analyze it the way we do today.

Of course, it was inevitable that interest in managerial style would grow in importance. Over the last 50 years, business leaders have had to function in a much more complicated and interdependent society. Today they must make decisions and exercise power in a landscape populated by stockholders, government agencies, labor laws, lobbying groups, politicians, journalists, trade unions, environmentalists, and, oh yes, attorneys.

Therefore, in our contemporary world we give a lot of thought to what it takes to direct, supervise, motivate, stimulate, inspire, compel, or otherwise influence people to accomplish the business of a corporation. An effective managerial style is valued as a key attribute. This is why business courses, books, and training seminars have been developed to help today's leaders cultivate a productive style.

DEFINING STYLE

While definitions vary, for the purpose of our discussion, let's define *managerial style* as the way managers interact, in speaking or behavior, with their coworkers—direct reports, peers, and superiors. It's the *how* of the equation—*how* they behave on a day-to-day basis as they conduct themselves with the people around them, taking in information, processing it, and making decisions.

All people in a position of leadership have a characteristic managerial style whether or not they recognize it. Certainly, if you work with a particular person for any length of time, you become aware of a set of behaviors that defines his or her style. Because human activity tends to evolve into predictable patterns, you see the same behaviors repeated often enough to identify them as representing an "autocratic," "supportive," "pragmatic," "easy-going," or "dominating" style, to name a few. Even when a manager's style is inconsistent, it is still a style. Coworkers will call it "erratic" or "unpredictable."

Today's successful executives consciously develop their managerial style. It is assumed to be an important element of effective leadership. And there is evidence to support this assumption. Decades of research show that managerial style actually has a significant effect on performance and productivity. Style matters.

There are conspicuous examples. When Lee Iacocca took over Chrysler during its crisis in the late 1970s, he had to make a series of smart and timely decisions to get his ailing corporation turned around. But is there any doubt about the vital role his style of management played in his ability to sell his plan to stockholders, his workforce, Congress, or the general public?

By all accounts, Walt Disney was a leader whose distinctive style was the driving force behind the visionary work his company did during his lifetime. Today it's hard to think of a business whose leaders are guided more directly in decision making by the spirit of their founder than the people at Disney—even though he died almost 40 years ago. Such has been his influence.

Virtually everyone acknowledges that New York Mayor Rudy Giuliani's style in taking charge after the 9/11 devastation set exactly the right tone for that city's quickly getting back to a semblance of normalcy.

Other figures with pronounced styles come to mind: Ted Turner, Rupert Murdoch, Donald Trump, Carli Fiorina, Ross Perot, and Oprah Winfrey. However, more instructive than citing examples is to make two points about style at any level of management that is borne out by research:

1. An effective managerial style can encourage high-quality performance from people.
2. A poor managerial style or one that's a mismatch for motivating people can foster mediocre or even poor performance.

You don't need to look to famous illustrations to substantiate these conclusions. Consider your own experience. Most people can point to personal examples where the particular style of a leader had a strong positive or negative effect on their performance. The more positive feelings we have at work in response to our boss's style, the more likely we will approach our work with energy and enthusiasm. When a style puts us off or affects us negatively, the more likely our work will suffer.

Later in this book we will describe a style of behavior that has proven highly effective for managers and has been used successfully throughout the corporate world.

STYLE IS NOT ENOUGH

It is ironic to be making such a strong case for the importance of style to your success as a manager. After all, the point of this chapter—indeed, of this book—is that while an effective style is essential, it is not enough to guarantee success.

Why not? Since style is about the manner we use in the workplace, it does not tell us directly as managers how we should spend our time or, more important, how direct reports should spend their time.

Another clue that indicates that style alone is not responsible for management success is that any number of managers may employ vastly different styles to achieve the same success. Therefore, it is difficult to derive from their styles the common denominators that would account for success for all leaders in all situations.

Understand that this is not an attempt to find a substitute for style. Because it is primarily a means to an end, however, your style does not accomplish any business goal in and of itself. It does not create success. Ultimately, your style has to serve on behalf of some business objective. It has to help you to get things done!

Chapter 1 pointed out that despite supposedly doing everything right to succeed, well-meaning managers feel frustrated that they are not getting the things done they should and certainly not fast enough. We also noted ironically that even at today's seemingly frenzied pace, a majority of working people themselves feel that they are underutilized. If today's emphasis on management style doesn't seem to be able to fix these problems, it's time to look beyond style. The job of managing may require style, but it requires much more as well.

Managing requires thinking ahead, framing issues properly, generating alternatives, and having good decision-making procedures, among other skills. And it requires maximizing the use of the people in your organization.

SEPARATING THE NOISE FROM THE SIGNAL

If style won't get you to the kind of performance you need, what do successful managers have in common that will? One factor is the ability to *focus* exclusively on the vital tasks of their organization and then to skillfully match these with the right people to complete them. Speaking about this quality in several notable leaders, George M. C. Fisher, chairman and CEO of Eastman Kodak, called it ". . . an ability to sort out the noise from the signal and then to drive just for the essence of what's important."

TO SORT OUT THE NOISE FROM THE SIGNAL

This first step recognizes an important task from all the unimportant possibilities that compete for attention. This is a cognitive skill you can develop that allows you to apply deliberation and judgment to your decisions about what work should be done.

TO DRIVE JUST FOR THE ESSENCE OF WHAT'S IMPORTANT

The second step essential for focusing is execution. For our purposes, the *drive* means assigning the task to the right person. Match what has to be done with the person or persons who have the experience and the technical, functional, interpersonal, and decision-making skills that are needed.

It is important to note, though, that this is not about selecting people. We assume that you have the right people in the right jobs. Our concern is how you use these people.

The tool to help you to focus and perform these management skills more effectively is the subject of the next chapter, the *task management model.*

CHAPTER 3

THE TASK MANAGEMENT MODEL

It is only in our decisions that we are important.

JEAN-PAUL SARTRE,
PHILOSOPHER

The basis of the proven system for getting the right things done is the *task management model.*

A *model* is a framework for organizing the "stuff" that is going on out there in the real world, a way to pin down what is happening and examine it in a coherent manner. The task management model will enable you to analyze any work assignment to discover the best way to approach it and the best people to assign to it so that it is done quickly and correctly.

THREE QUESTIONS TO ASK FOR EVERY WORK ASSIGNMENT

There are three broad dimensions to think about each and every time you assign work if you want to ensure that the right things are getting done.

FIRST DIMENSION: IS THE TASK IMPORTANT?

Numerous books and articles have discussed this first concern. But this is merely the starting point. It is the "gatekeeper" question. It is included because if a task isn't important, nothing else matters. Only if it first passes the importance test and gets through the gate should you think about assigning it.

Determining if a task is important forces you to focus. And even when you use all your analytical skills to decide, circumstances can change quickly. You know how turbulent the workplace can be. Today's priorities may be irrelevant tomorrow. And the cost can be high for not changing, for not continually asking what is important.

The Internet is a good example. Only 10 years ago most businesspeople hadn't even heard the terms *e-business* and *e-commerce*. The first commercial Web sites were used merely as online brochures. From those humble beginnings, annual sales on the Web are already enormous, topping $45 billion within a decade. Woe to the company that didn't make the Internet a top priority in that time period. For nearly every enterprise it quickly became an important task to develop a Web site and be represented. Even when a company decided not to participate, it was still important to make that decision and develop marketing strategies to counter Internet competition. One thing is certain: The Web has challenged most business executives to evaluate continually what is important to do in this area.

Now expand this kind of questioning to all areas of your job as manager. Shouldn't every task you assign be important? Imagine a coach assigning "work" that isn't important to his players during a game. Suppose that a football coach tells a lineman on the field to start counting the number of people in the stands or begin working on a history of the team while he's out there. Or think of an orchestra conductor telling the oboe player, "Just do what you feel comfortable with, and try to keep busy until the end of the symphony."

While these analogies are outlandish, managers are often guilty of getting this far off track from the important tasks. Are you assigning or allowing some of your people to do the equivalent of counting the crowd at a football game when truly important work needs to be done on your playing field?

To be fair, knowing what is important is usually more complicated for a business manager than for a sports coach or an orchestra conductor. To help define importance, let's lay down some basics that apply to any commercial enterprise. *Important* means that:

1. The task clearly helps to drive the performance and achieve the business and financial goals of the organization.

2. If the task doesn't get done, it will hurt the performance of the organization.

3. It is urgent (needs to be done now).

Of course, while these requirements provide direction, they still need your ongoing interpretation.

Think of the importance of a task as the first concern or dimension of task management, a continuum along which any assignment you make can be rated objectively all the way from *unnecessary* to a *must-do* task. How would you rate the work you assign and the work your people are already doing? Go over all the decisions you made at work yesterday, for instance, and ask yourself how they rate.

Since many management books and seminars stop at this point, they only address decisions managers make about *what* they assign people to do. Often this takes the form of setting work priorities or finding ways to speed up the process. Task management isn't about prioritizing work or managing time. What makes this model unique is its emphasis on *how* you make assignments. *Who* do you choose? You must take into account two additional dimensions that are vital for any perceptive management decision.

SECOND DIMENSION: IS THE PERSON CAPABLE OF DOING THE TASK?

You would be surprised by the number of managers who do not know their direct reports well enough to evaluate who should get a particular assignment. Or who don't understand the importance. How well do you know your people? Are you assigning work by habit or from a thorough knowledge of their strengths and weaknesses?

For instance, it is amazing the number of assignments that are given to people incapable of doing them. A manager may even know it when she makes the assignment! However, if capability is not something you consider when you assign work, it should be.

Understand, this does not mean that you have the wrong people. No one is perfect for every job. We all have gaps in our experience, blind spots, and biases.

To focus more accurately on what it means to be capable, here are several criteria to address when considering a direct report for a task. He or she should have:

1. The technical and functional expertise to do the task.
2. The problem-solving and decision-making skills to do the task.
3. The interpersonal skills to do the task.

Ideally, the person under consideration would have a full measure of all three. However, this is hardly ever the case. You have to determine what degree of each element is needed most for the particular task you have in mind. If you want someone to design an e-mail system or plan a budget, expertise will be more important than the other two. If you need someone to work on a customer profile or head up a committee to extend your product line, you may want someone who has a large measure of the second and third skills.

While it may seem obvious that you'll get the best results by matching the task that needs to be done with the most capable person, why isn't this done every single time work is assigned? What gets in the way?

The biggest culprit is the organization chart. A slavish devotion to following the chain of command and job titles can put an important job assignment in the wrong hands.

The next biggest offender is poor or lazy planning. Some people are assigned certain jobs because the tasks in question are viewed as being their responsibility or because they have always gotten those jobs. This occurs despite changes in personnel that have brought in people who may be more skilled or have a better background and more training.

Some managers mistake keeping everyone busy for getting a lot accomplished. For them, once again, the organization chart or the schedule is king, whether or not it makes sense. They make snap judgments that have everyone doing something immediately to keep everybody busy. They don't step back and examine the best fit of task to person. The incessant schedule makers tend to assign the same tasks to the same people all the time. Or they assign them to the first available people.

Then there are managers who like to keep everyone happy. They are reluctant to challenge a contented employee with a difficult task, even if that person would have the best shot at succeeding. They don't want to rock the boat or risk a negative reaction as a result of giving someone increased responsibility.

Notice that there's an interplay between these variables. This is because *task importance* and *employee capability* affect each other. For example, suppose that the head of the legal department allows the highest qualified attorneys to work on matters outside their expertise or assigns them inconsequential work. Because of his own lack of analysis or poor planning, important work that comes in later may be assigned by default to those who are available but less capable. As you can see, the fault here isn't with the staff. It's how the work is assigned.

As with *task importance*, you can view *employee capability* as a continuum from an *incapable* person to a *capable* person. In reality, the extremes are even more pronounced. The worst incapable person for a particular task will be an inept bungler, and the best capable person is probably an expert.

Now let's add the third and final dimension of task management.

THIRD DIMENSION: DOES THE PERSON ENJOY THE TASK?

As managers, if we were only making decisions for a workforce of robots in a factory, we could stop at the first two dimensions discussed. Simply define the task, size up the capability of the machine, and put it on the job. The final dimension factors in the broad spectrum of human nature and emotion.

We would be poor managers indeed if we overlooked the human element because it can influence results dramatically. Even if we could guarantee that only important work would be assigned to capable people, we would still not have 100 percent productivity. We can't ignore asking whether or not a person assigned to a task will enjoy it.

It is a well-known behavioral principle that people who like their work do a better job. Not only has psychological testing proven this, but common sense also tells us that this is true. Enjoying a task brings out good feelings that translate into energy and enthusiasm. People roll up their sleeves and dive in. You often can't hold back someone who loves her work.

Here are three principles to keep in mind about *employee enjoyment:*

1. It is the product of positive feelings and emotions.
2. It is not related to facts or logic. (Therefore, it is subjective rather than objective.)
3. It is based on the pleasure principle (defined below).

If it takes good judgment to rate the importance of tasks and the capability of people to do them, you might think it would require a psychic to predict what tasks people will enjoy. Why is it in an advertising agency, for example, that the creative staff regard the accountants as the "bean counters," while the accountants think of the creative people as the "whackos"? There is no easy answer for why some people get enjoyment out of designing brochures and others find supreme satisfaction balancing a ledger.

Some of your direct reports may be happy as can be doing a very narrow noncreative task. Others may only turn on when let loose to come up with an ingenious solution to a problem. No doubt you have people who enjoy secure kinds of tasks with little risk involved. Others love the competitive arena and enjoy nothing better than a high-risk performance, such as landing a big client.

Managers can't be expected to understand the intricate personality characteristics that account for people's behavior. However, managers should get to know people's likes and dislikes. They should be able to predict with some accuracy which assignments a direct report will take and run with and which ones will be treated like poison. A way to ensure a good match for enjoyment is to get lots of feedback. Find out directly what people enjoy and what they don't.

As with the other variables, employees' enjoyment is on a continuum. This means that there is a downside to consider. If *enjoy* goes at one end, meaning ecstatic about doing a task, then at the other extreme is *despise* (or hating it). Most assignments fall somewhere in between.

What do you do with a capable person who is good at a task he despises? It may be surprising to think that this would be the case. After all, a good measure of enjoyment and satisfaction usually comes simply from doing something well, as noted earlier. It may be that within every organization there are certain tasks that almost everyone dislikes. Taking inventory is usually not enjoyable. Tax audits are no more fun for corporate accountants than they are for the rest of us. Somebody in the organization is usually very good at these tasks but doesn't necessarily enjoy them. In fact, the higher one rises in an organization, the more often one must tackle some highly disliked tasks because they are the responsibility of the people at the top. Dismissing employees is a good example. Or closing a plant.

As you can see, then, complications arise when making assignments in weighing the three variables. For instance, here's another balancing problem that comes up again and again. Enjoyment is based on the *pleasure principle.* Simply stated, this principle says that people are attracted to activities that make them feel good and avoid those that make them feel bad.

The problem is that people can end up spending time on a task they are not particularly good at but feel good doing. They're having fun! Or worse, they enjoy doing a task that has become completely unnecessary. Maybe it was relevant and vital at one time, but that time has long passed. This is the manager's dilemma.

Enjoyment has to be carefully balanced against the other dimensions. Managers have to be careful that they are not just feeding their own comfort levels by assigning familiar but unimportant tasks while avoiding new but relevant tasks that may provoke anxiety. We will discuss methods for building in satisfaction from doing important work that doesn't result in instant gratification.

To summarize, *task management* means analyzing any potential work assignment with these three dimensions in mind. Here again is each presented as a continuum between two extremes:

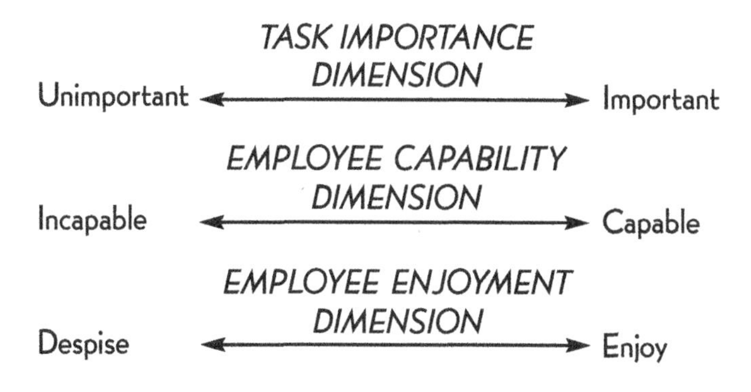

Now let's put them together in a visual way—as a cognitive map that will take the wide range of your decision making about the assignment and organize it so that you can make logical choices.

The first dimension, *task importance*, is placed to one side by itself. This should always be the first decision you make. Frankly, if your honest appraisal of a potential project or assignment tells you that it isn't important for your company to be doing, then you shouldn't be interested in how well it gets done or if people enjoy it. It's wasting valuable time and energy. Thus *importance* is the prerequisite for the rest of the analysis.

Once it is determined that a task is worth doing, that it is in the top part of the importance scale, you can see what the task management model looks like in its entirety (see page 31).

When you consider who you should choose for a task, you can calculate roughly where it falls on the grid of five possibilities (A through E) based on an intersection of the dimensions. A few general observations about the model will help to orient you. As mentioned earlier, *task importance* has been separated, up and down, as your first consideration.

A. When tasks fail the *importance* test, they all go in one place—the *basement* (bottom box). It is called this because these activities shouldn't see the light of day. They don't contribute to getting the right things done. Over time, the goal is to make sure that no one is working in the basement. We want to bring people upstairs doing the *vital* work of the organization.

THE DIMENSIONS OF TASK MANAGEMENT

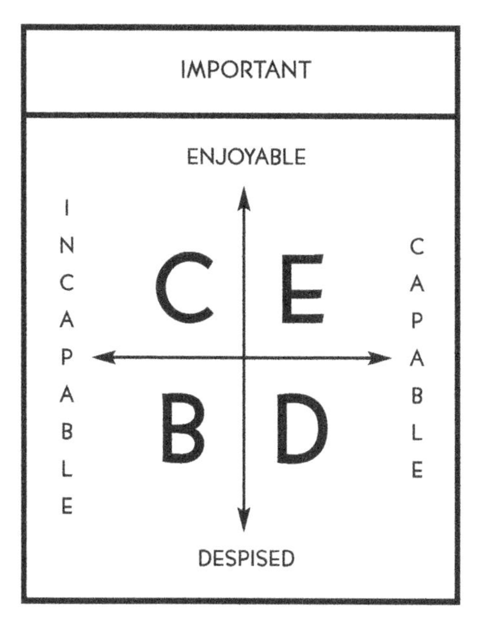

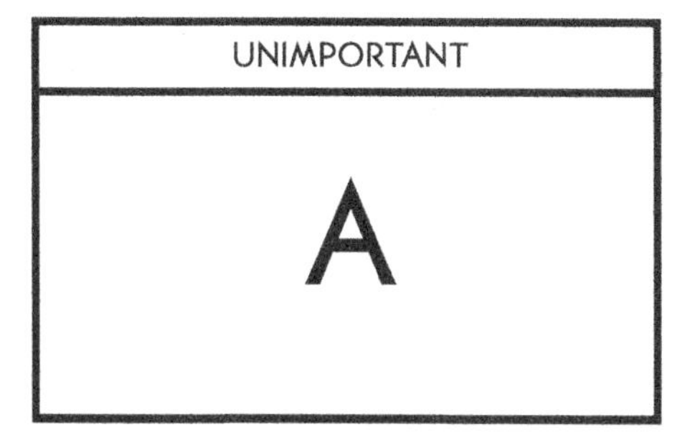

All important tasks are represented above the basement level. The two remaining dimensions, *capability* and *enjoyment*, are the axes for the grid. Because these activities are at the heart of the organization's success, they should be assigned carefully and thoughtfully so that the right people are doing them. Since there is no question that *somebody* in the organization should be carrying out these important tasks, let's focus on the interplay of these two dimensions.

B. As a manager, if you assign necessary work to direct reports who *aren't capable* and are *not excited* by the task, you are asking for trouble. Motivation will be low. Even if people are dragged into overcoming their loathing to get the task done, the result likely will be poor because of the mismatch between their skills and the nature of the task. The logical outcome of a job assignment in this position is a long delay, a quick but half-hearted attempt, or a botched mess.

C. This task goes to someone *enthused* about doing it but who is *not capable*. Because the job is important, if the employee does it poorly, it will have to be done over or reassigned. Sometimes a manager has no choice but to use a particular direct report for the task. Often it is desirable as a growth opportunity. Because there is enthusiasm and a willingness to learn, it is possible to make this assignment a success by giving the employee assistance in any of several ways.

Finally, we come to the part of the model in which capable people are assigned important work. Enjoyment is the only variable.

D. Why would a manager assign a task to a *capable* employee who will *hate doing it?* If it is an important task, he may have no choice. *Somebody* has to do it. That person could be the best or only one for the job. It was mentioned earlier that tasks such as taking inventory or representing a company during an audit are often necessary but not beloved. Making staff or budget cuts is almost always a detested job that is required from time to time. To muster an excellent performance from must-do tasks that an employee doesn't like will require ingenuity on the part of the manager. She needs to oversee the project closely and offer incentives to coax an energetic turnaround.

E. In a perfect world managers would always assign important work to *capable* employees who *find fulfillment and enjoyment from it.* For a manager striving to get the right things done, this is a worthy goal to shoot for every day.

Think of the potential that could be tapped if you attempted to make every work assignment a meaningful one, out of the basement. Then, from knowing your people well, envision matching that assignment to the people whose skills and talents are the ones needed to do the best job. Beyond that, if these well-matched employees were energized by the satisfaction they would get from working on a task they like, you would have an extraordinary burst of productivity, a big spike in performance.

You don't have to cross your fingers or get lucky to move toward the upper right of the task management model. By keeping the dynamics of the three variables in mind and using the model as a practical guide to apply on the job, you can systematically go about doing what it takes to make successful management decisions. Furthermore, by applying the model to management decisions that you anticipate making, you can avoid mistakes that keep the right things from getting done by the right people.

FROM BLACK HOLES TO GOLD STARS

Now that you have some familiarity with the model, let's designate each area with a simple icon to make it easier to remember and for reference (see page 35).

At the top, then, is the matrix of important jobs with the same *employee capability* and *employee enjoyment* variables but with new names for these tasks:

Gold stars. Capable people doing important work who enjoy it. What's a better term for the task that has it all?

Big Ds. They are big Ds because they are important tasks that capable people must do even though they dislike them. The D is for *discipline.* It takes discipline to get these done. They provide a particular challenge for the manager who must assign them (possibly presenting the manager with his own big D).

THE TASK MANAGEMENT MODEL

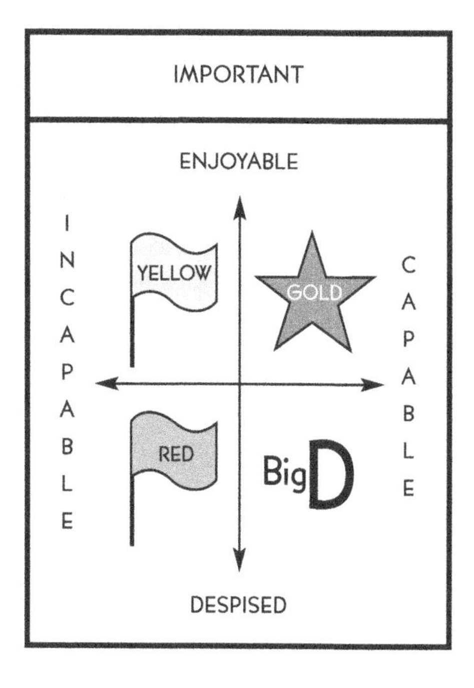

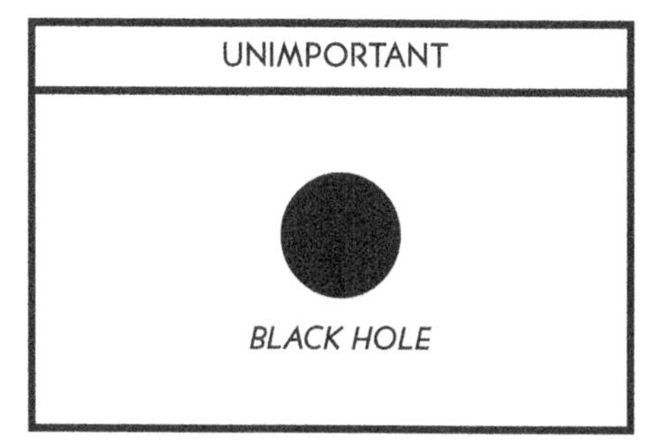

Yellow flags. Important tasks that are given to enthusiastic people who lack the capability to do them should be a yellow flag of caution to the manager. They are a signal that the manager must provide a way for people to attain the complementary skills needed to achieve a good result.

Red flags. Important work that has to be done is being assigned to incapable people who don't want to do it. This situation is a signal to stop and reconsider. It can only bring trouble.

Black holes. All assignments here are unimportant. Since these tasks don't contribute to getting the right things done, when people perform black hole activities, it puts them—and possibly keeps them—in the basement. The focused manager's goal is to eliminate them altogether.

Like black holes in space that suck in all the light and energy around them, black hole tasks suck in the time and energy of employees who will continue doing them forever if someone doesn't step in and recognize that no bottom-line purpose for the company is being served. Some organizations use up a lot of time pursuing them without questioning their purpose.

YOU MAKE THE CALL

Now that you are familiar with the task management model, let's apply it to some management decisions for analysis. (To simplify the situation in order to make a point, let's assume that there are no personal problems between the managers and their direct reports in these examples. Assume also that the managerial style in each case is not a factor that is interfering with performance. Life isn't this simple, of course, but these assumptions help us to focus on one thing at a time.)

> Dave heads up the sales department of a company that makes wholesale paper products. One of his direct reports, Lois, does quite a bit of telemarketing. She often complains to Dave that the product information sheets she sends out to prospects need serious updating. Some of the item numbers have changed, and some products have been discontinued. Dave agrees, but he has not had a printing budget large enough to get them overhauled—until this year.
>
> Therefore, 3 months ago he told Lois the exciting news and put her in charge of updating the product sheets. Since then, she has done virtually nothing on the project. When he asks about it, she talks vaguely about not getting to it yet. She's still sending out the old product sheets but has stopped complaining. Dave doesn't understand. He thought that of all people, Lois would be the one motivated to move this job along. This is why he assigned it to her!

Does Dave's assignment fall into one of the five areas of the model? Evaluate the three dimensions, starting with importance.

How does the job rate? Should the product sheets be updated? Is this a worthwhile task? Of course it is. The product sheets are important for the salespeople of the company. They communicate vital and specific information that can help make the sale. If they aren't up to date and are sent to potential customers with corrections made by hand, they leave a bad impression of the company.

Dave got in trouble, however, on the next two variables when he assigned the job to Lois. He mistook her enthusiasm to have new product sheets as a good reason to put her in charge of the project. However, he should have asked himself: Is Lois capable of overseeing the production of a product sheet? There is no reason to think that she is. She's a salesperson, not a production manager.

Let's assume that the reason she didn't get anywhere on the project is that she was out of her element. Dave assigned the task to someone who is not capable of doing it, at least not to the minimum standards expected at a reputable company.

Normally, this might seem to be a simple matter of Lois saying to Dave, "Hey, I don't know anything about putting out sales literature!" However, Lois might feel sheepish reacting in this way. She's the one who pressed her boss. Now he has given her what she wants. She would hate to disappoint him. She tells herself that she will talk to other people and learn how to put together a product information sheet.

However, when she starts asking around, Lois finds that there's a lot more to the task than she thought. New photographs will have to be taken of products, and she doesn't know a thing about hiring a photographer, how much they charge, or how to set up a shooting session. She doesn't know much about printers and printing either. The more questions she asks, the more complicated it seems. And she has no idea how much to spend on it. She does what a lot of people do who are afraid of getting in over their heads. She avoids the whole thing—lying low and hoping that maybe it will go away.

This leads us to the third variable. Dave didn't consider if Lois would enjoy overseeing the production of a new product information sheet. If she were capable of doing it, it might not matter. It would have to be done, like it or not. However, had Dave been appraising her enjoyment level, he may have asked her if she would like to do it and found out, incidentally, that she was incapable.

For Lois, therefore, this project is either a red flag or a yellow flag. The difference between the two is that we really don't know her attitude toward the task. Let's say that she hates it right from the start. Perhaps a previous bad experience has taught her that she shouldn't go near a printing project. In such a case, the decision to assign her this task without sizing up her capability or knowing her likes or dislikes has two strikes against it. As the example shows, a real-life Lois might avoid the project altogether and never get it done.

What if Lois's case is a yellow flag? Suppose that she was excited to undertake the project, feeling that she could be the driving force in getting new product information sheets. As indicated earlier, however, her lack of skills in this area eventually could dampen her enthusiasm and leave her feeling hopelessly bogged down.

Many yellow flags cannot be avoided but have the benefit of providing a learning and growth experience. Therefore, if Dave tries to help Lois, this yellow flag doesn't have to be a washout. Dave might hire an outside art director to work with her. If there is no budget for that and no one else is available on the inside to handle the production, Dave might team her with someone in the company who can share knowledge and experience. Dave may still keep Lois in charge of the project, but he has to understand that it could take longer this time around. He also may have to work closely with Lois to keep her on track, breaking the job down into steps that can be monitored to finish it successfully.

Remember, yellow flag tasks have to be done. If they can't be reassigned as someone else's gold star or big D, there are tactics to make them a success. The key is for the manager to understand the situation. The purpose for thinking about an assignment in terms of the model is to get you to focus deliberately on the factors at play that will work for you or against you. You can judge in advance the likelihood of the job getting done. If the likelihood is low, you should do something about it. Change the task itself, assign it to a different person, or decide how you may have to help arrange for success.

Let's look at a more complex example, one that incorporates a number of management decisions as part of an ongoing project.

Howard is marketing director for a national manufacturer of eyeglass frames. He works hard and has an excellent staff that he has put together over a number of years. His corporation's objective over the next 5 years is to reach a younger market for the designer eyewear the company makes instead of the traditional upscale, older consumers with more discretionary income to spend. How can the company reach younger adults and convince them to upgrade their frame purchases?

Howard welcomes his staff's ideas for shifting their traditional media outlets to more youth-oriented ones: music and fashion magazines, the Internet, MTV, and radio. Howard also feels that his company's presence at nontraditional venues for eyewear, such as sponsorship of selected sporting events, music concerts, and youth-oriented festivals around the country, is a good strategy too.

All these efforts will be aimed at driving potential customers to retail locations or to a newly conceived Web site. Howard envisions that by uploading a digital snapshot of his or her face, a prospect can "try on" his company's frames in a virtual way before actually visiting a store.

Many members of Howard's staff are enthusiastic, especially the younger ones, excited about being assigned to buy time on MTV or place ads in hot new magazines. Unfortunately, most of their previous contacts for placing ads are of little help in making deals with the new media. They make a lot of mistakes and don't get the best ad placement or rates.

Howard has two staff members who have experience buying radio time. They spend a good deal of time putting together a radio time-buying package. The problem is that they soon realize that it makes little sense to sell a product with so much visual appeal on radio, particularly in light of the other marketing ideas and budget limits for the entire project.

Howard becomes frustrated in his other efforts. While he holds lots of planning meetings to research and choose events for program advertising, signage, booths, and so on for his company's eyewear, a lot of the follow-through never happens. Howard knows that everyone is going through a steep learning curve to find these new outlets, but he is still disappointed that so often they miss deadlines for being at this music event or that festival. Yet this is an area that several people practically begged him to work on.

One of his staff members loves using the Internet. So Howard assigns that part of the project to her. However, since she doesn't have much technical experience, early meetings with the company's Web designers are frustrating. It is difficult to understand some of the technical problems the designers foresee in developing the idea. The timetable for a prototype to test

> keeps moving closer to the actual marketing launch.
>
> Finally, although Howard has had high hopes for the sporting event tie-ins, such as the U.S. Open Tennis Tournament, he comes up short. He chose that project himself because of his personal interest in tennis. However, he has so much else to do and his personal knowledge of sports marketing is so weak that he abandons the idea. It is ironic because he doesn't even realize that a member of his own staff has had sports marketing experience in her previous job.

What happened to Howard? While exaggerated to illustrate a variety of poor management decisions, this example shows how the failure to think through each work assignment of a project can drag down an entire department. This should be a vibrant group running on all cylinders. Instead, it's chugging along at half speed and failing to deliver.

Have you determined the kinds of tasks on the task management grid that Howard was assigning? What did he do to sabotage his efforts without realizing it until it was too late?

BLACK HOLES

For the purposes of discussion, let's assume that the strategy for reaching a younger audience was sound. Thus Howard made correct choices about the importance of the assignments he was making—with one notable exception.

We mentioned that some of his people spent a considerable amount of time putting together an advertising plan for radio when early on it was obvious that radio did not make much sense. It didn't fit the product, the budget, or the ambitious goals for the rest of the marketing plan. Therefore, Howard's people were doing some black hole work. As is often the case, if employees happen to enjoy black hole tasks, they may just keep doing them unless they are called off. Howard should have reassigned them to do something much more vital. Because he didn't, their effort was wasted, and Howard could have used them working on other areas of the project.

YELLOW FLAGS

Howard's people were excited about their new assignments, such as buying television time and finding music events and festivals to sponsor. However, without providing the necessary follow-through to enable his people to have the skills needed for their new tasks, Howard was guilty of giving yellow flag assignments and walking away from them. There was too much at stake in this case for a "fend for yourselves" approach.

While it is normally good for people to learn and grow on the job, this was not a peripheral or experimental project for which Howard's department had the luxury to experience failure for any length of time. His company was expecting the marketing effort to jump-start itself. Howard's department needed to make smart decisions about unfamiliar media and entirely new marketing venues.

Rather than setting his people adrift to sink or swim, Howard should have done everything to ensure that sinking would not be an option. This is not always easy when direct reports are enthusiastic and ready to jump into a project they aren't prepared for.

RED FLAGS

The Web site project was assigned to a staff member who enjoys using the Internet. This guaranteed that this person was familiar with retailing on the Web. However, it didn't mean that she knew or understood any of the intricacies of Web design. It turns out that she didn't like any of the technical aspects of using a computer. An initial enthusiasm quickly turned to, at best, a lack of enthusiasm for this task due in part to lengthy discussions with the Web designers over technical issues.

What could Howard have done to avoid the yellow and red flags? The answer is very similar to Dave's in the first example. Howard should have known his people well enough and asked the right questions to evaluate accurately what skills and knowledge his staff members actually had for the new program. He could have teamed knowledgeable members with those who needed help in order to share information and show them the ropes. If his entire department was lacking, which it appears to have been in certain areas, he could have looked outside for help, either in other areas of his company or through consultants who would teach staff members their new roles. He might have hired several new people permanently as well, given that the entire marketing approach changed so radically.

GOLD STARS

Of particular interest in this example is how Howard muffed the opportunity for his product to be a U.S. Open Tennis Tournament sponsor. Howard made a significant mistake by not finding out that he had someone on his staff with sports marketing experience. The reason in this case is that he did something managers may be tempted to do. He kept a glamour assignment for himself. The pleasure principle was seducing him. When faced with a number of unpleasant tasks, particularly big Ds, it is always tempting to spend time on something more fun. In this case, since he wasn't qualified to do the job, he should have given it to someone else. In fact, in bypassing someone with marketing experience on his staff, he missed the opportunity to turn this yellow flag for himself into a gold star for one of his people.

Overall, then, while it may appear to Howard that he wasn't served well by his staff, perhaps they weren't served well by Howard as a manager. Had he managed better, he would have given his employees what they needed to do the best possible job. Enabling people is assigning them power and authority but also giving them the means to develop or obtain the competencies they need to get things done.

Chapter 4 will present more examples as we discuss specifically five common errors managers make in assigning work that undermines their efforts to accomplish tasks.

To get you thinking about the effect a pattern of poorly thought-out management decisions can have on an organization, here are several questions. Consider the behavior described as occurring over a period of at least a year. What happens in a workplace where a manager

- Habitually delegates tasks she is capable of doing to direct reports who are incapable?
- Habitually assigns big D tasks to the same people all the time?
- Frequently assigns unimportant tasks that are enjoyable?
- Frequently assigns unimportant tasks that are disliked?
- Delegates red flag tasks to her direct reports?
- Keeps the gold star assignments for herself?

CHAPTER 4

FIVE COMMON MANAGEMENT ERRORS THAT KEEP YOU FROM GETTING THINGS DONE

Victory often goes to the army that makes the least mistakes, not the most brilliant plans.

CHARLES DE GAULLE,
GENERAL AND PRESIDENT OF FRANCE

Now that you are familiar with the task management model and have had some practice applying it, let's move the discussion closer to home.

You are dissatisfied with the productivity of the people you manage. You think that it could be higher. You are probably right—if for no other reason than the point made in Chapter 1 that a majority of the workforce is not achieving its potential on the job.

Once again, it is important to note that this is not about people selection. While choosing the right personnel is critical, our starting point is to assume that you have the right people in the right positions. However, everyone has strengths and weaknesses, likes and dislikes, and areas of responsibility where they have little or no experience.

Our contention is that many of the managing problems that interfere with productivity stem from habitual thinking or not thinking at all. Managers routinely bypass the cognitive process that makes each decision a product of sound reasoning. Yet making a decision about assigning work can be done in a completely disciplined way. If there's one basic principle behind the task management model, it is that you can break down decisions rationally to focus on the best course of action.

Even knowing this, managers still fail. We are all human. We still make bad decisions about what's important work and who should do it because we give in to custom or to our own habitual way of doing things. Or we have a knee-jerk reaction that stops us from analyzing people and circumstances. All of these can derail the thinking process.

With this in mind, this chapter identifies five errors managers make most often that keep them from getting the right things done. Most of them have been mentioned already in explaining the model. However, the model isn't merely a way to locate and label work assignments. The purpose of thinking in terms of the model's three dimensions is to provide a fresh way of looking at management decisions and thus to cultivate insight and foresight about assigning work.

Therefore, as the errors are presented, be brutally honest and ask yourself if any of these behaviors is keeping you from separating the noise from the signal. They are presented roughly in the order of how frequently they occur.

1. ALLOWING BLACK HOLE ACTIVITIES TO TAKE PLACE

As you know, black hole activities are all unimportant work in an organization. It doesn't matter if employees like them or hate them. It doesn't matter if they do them well or do them poorly. It's all going on in the basement, sapping time and productivity from the company.

If you are guilty of assigning busy work, trivial tasks, or unimportant time wasters to your direct reports, you should ask yourself why. What possible benefit can there be for your organization or yourself now or in the long run to clutter the workday with meaningless activity?

Several reasons have been mentioned already. Some managers mistake keeping everyone busy for getting things done. Giving an incompetent employee something meaningless to do may be preferable to the more difficult task of dismissing him. At least he's out of harm's way. And maybe, after awhile, he'll quit on his own.

Giving an employee a meaningless task may be a way of demeaning or punishing her. The manager says to himself, "I'll teach Sharon a lesson for not supporting me in front of the boss. I'll make her put together a bunch of tedious reports that I'll just ignore when she turns them in. She'll get the message about who she should be loyal to in the future."

This thinking is the kind of games playing that borders on abuse. No matter what the motivation, though, the remedy is simple: Stop assigning this kind of work immediately. You are hurting your company, and you are ultimately shooting yourself in the foot if you make these kinds of assignments—for whatever reason.

However, let's assume that your very interest in being a more productive manager precludes your consciously *assigning* unimportant work. As it is stated, the error is *allowing* black hole activities. This is a more difficult problem to perceive and to overcome.

First, as you know, what constitutes an *important* activity may fluctuate widely. Circumstances can change quickly within an industry, making what was important yesterday irrelevant today. After all, a fundamental attribute of a successful, competitive business is to change quickly to meet new circumstances or opportunities.

For instance, the mandate from Congress to convert entirely from conventional television to digital has changed the priorities of television manufacturers for years to come. Besides legislation, scientific discoveries, legal rulings, industry consolidation, and the threat of terrorism are just some of the ways outside forces can change the landscape.

Assuming, though, that as a manager you have your finger on the pulse of what is the important work to be done, how do black hole projects slip through and even continue, day after day, year after year?

THE MANAGER DOESN'T KNOW ABOUT THEM

The more people she has working for her, the more likely this will be true. This is why a good manager can't be chained to her desk or aloof from her people. She needs to be interested in the work being done and ask a lot of questions. It is not always a matter of employees "getting away with" doing unimportant work. They may not realize it themselves!

For instance, the accounting department of a long-established brokerage house circulates reams of internal reports that have long been outmoded. Nobody reads or uses them. This is black hole territory.

A publishing company routinely distributes its manuscripts to four different proofreaders even though technology has eliminated many of the typographical errors that once were prevalent. After two proofreaders, the activity is redundant.

A senior executive for a local drugstore chain realizes that he can never talk with a store manager on a Tuesday afternoon because all the managers attend a standing meeting on that day every week. This has been the custom for as long as anyone can remember. After investigating their meeting agendas, the executive discovers that every topic could be handled easily by fax or e-mail because every store is now computerized. While contact among these managers is valuable, the executive cuts their meetings to once a month or "as needed."

You can see that to root out the black hole activities going on around her that she doesn't know about, a manager has to constantly question the value of all activities and analyze their worth. It not only requires that she know what is important, she also has to have a good understanding of how people spend their time.

THE MANAGER ISN'T DISCIPLINED ENOUGH TO STOP THEM

If a manager doesn't have a crystal-clear idea of what he wants to accomplish, he may allow people to continue doing meaningless activities because he doesn't know how to redirect their efforts. If he is insecure about making decisions, the vacuum his indecision creates may become inhabited with black holes.

This is a difficult position to be in. It requires a lot of discipline to blow the whistle and stop contented employees from doing something even though it is a waste of time. And black holes can occur at any level in an organization.

For instance, suppose that a senior finance vice president for a regional sporting goods chain traditionally makes semiannual road trips to all the stores. They have had no consequence to the success of the company. They don't add to his already vast knowledge or help him do a better job. The store personnel don't benefit either.

So why does the vice president do it? It's a ritual he enjoys. He has always done it. Of course, when the chain was much smaller, he could accomplish it in a couple of days. Now it takes a week or more. And while he is gone, important work may pile up on his desk. Projects linger that need his hands-on attention. Decisions are put off because his input is important. It's also a black hole for the store managers. While they have to play host to an important visitor, they are taken away from the numerous tasks needing their attention at their stores.

His boss should counsel this executive that he's needed at headquarters too much to be roaming the countryside. But it's a difficult thing to tell a senior executive. It becomes a big D task for the boss, who may decide not to address the problem.

Consider the whole area of pet projects. Many may have dubious goals for the company and detract severely from the real work of the organization getting done. The research and development division of a manufacturing company has legitimate work to do. At any given time, though, it may have a project or two for a new product that the company hasn't the remotest chance of developing. The idea may be in a category for which the company doesn't even have any expertise. Yet people are working on it. Perhaps it began as a black hole the manager didn't know about. Now there's so much time and money invested that it has taken on a life of its own. It will be extremely difficult for a manager to close down this kind of project, but this is just what she should do.

You can see why this is the most prevalent error of the five. First, it is not always easy to recognize what's going on. Then it can be difficult to apply the correct solution. Nevertheless, black holes should be stopped as soon as they are identified.

It's important here to make a distinction: Just because a manager is unaware of an activity, it isn't automatically a black hole. In any organization, work is going on unknown to managers that is or will be important and valuable. Those in charge have to be careful to see the difference and not stifle creativity or initiative.

2. PAYING TOO LITTLE ATTENTION TO YELLOW FLAG ACTIVITIES

Now let's move out of the basement to the other four errors, all of which center on activity that is important to an organization. The most common for managers is yellow flags.

Managers can make two kinds of yellow flag errors. Both are the result of not thinking about exactly what skills are needed by the person who is assigned a task. A direct report's eagerness to jump in and tackle a job may obscure everyone's thinking. Yet how can a skill deficiency not be a profound detriment to getting things done?

The first yellow flag mistake a manager can make is the more obvious: By giving little thought about what her people are good at doing, she turns what might be gold star tasks for the right people into yellow flags by assigning them to the wrong people. She needlessly tries to make square pegs fit into round holes.

For instance, an executive of a bank wants to fill an important slot for a big project. Perhaps the bank needs to formulate new guidelines for promotions and pay raises. He picks one of his best managers, Martha, who did such a great job streamlining paperwork at all the branches. He figures that her intelligence and leadership on one project make her a prime candidate for the other. He doesn't understand that it was Martha's ability to analyze systems that allowed her to excel. She is great at that kind of work. However, she's not a people person, and this project requires interviewing lots of people about evaluations and performance.

Martha's assignment is a yellow flag for her. She has a capability gap for the human resources aspects of this project. She also has no background to bring to it. If she's smart, she may figure out how to overcome her deficiency, but her boss is not playing to her strengths. In fact, what compounds the mistake is that Ruth, a talented employee in the human resources department, could be a better person for this new project. It would be her gold star if the boss were assessing his people correctly.

Another example: Everett, the senior accountant for an advertising agency, has been tapped by his boss to determine what his firm's corporate charity project will be this year. He feels good about the task, but he doesn't know a thing about the subject. Hardly anyone likes his final choice, which is a shame.

His boss picked him because the task involved money, and Everett's his top accountant. Actually, if she were honest, Everett's boss would have to admit that she didn't give much thought at all to assigning this task. If she had, she would have remembered that Everett only came to the community a year ago. Therefore, he has little knowledge of the charities in town. Besides, an advertising agency usually has lots of creative, involved people around who would be plugged into that kind of thing. A few moments of thought would have put this yellow flag on the desk of someone who would have handled it quickly as his or her gold star.

What can you as a manager do to keep from needlessly assigning yellow flags? You should know your people's strengths and weaknesses. And this doesn't mean only their job qualifications or skills. It goes beyond that to discovering their likes and dislikes and their talents. You don't want to have any lights hiding under bushels among your staff.

Next, you have to be vigilant about thinking through the assignments you give. It can't be said enough: Managing means thinking about your decisions. Keep asking yourself, "Is this a yellow flag for this direct report? Could it be someone else's gold star?" We'll have more to say about gold stars shortly.

Now let's talk about the second kind of error managers make with yellow flags. It occurs when a yellow flag assignment is unavoidable. And there are a lot of situations where yellow flags *are* desirable.

Almost all personal growth comes from taking on a yellow flag task. People are eager and motivated to do something new, but they are not capable yet. Job promotions have many characteristics of a yellow flag. You are asking someone to step into a new role that's not totally familiar. If the shoe buyer for a department store retires after 20 years, his replacement is not likely to match that kind of experience. He won't know the subtleties of that position for a while.

The changing nature of business itself may require people to take on new tasks for which they are not completely qualified. A merger is an event in which lots of people can have new roles. Downsizing may require people to double up their duties. Something as simple as covering an illness may require someone to step into a yellow flag situation.

You can't just hire or fire someone every time change occurs in your organization. Therefore, you must continually determine how to deploy the strengths and weaknesses of the people you have. And unlike black holes, which you should try to pluck out of your organization like dandelions, a yellow flag task *must* be performed. It is an important activity.

The second kind of error is this: neglecting to give the person assigned a yellow flag the help needed to succeed.

Let's return to the bank example. We know that Martha is not the person for the job. It's not a good fit. Suppose that it turns out that no one person is really well qualified to take on the promotions project, but Jim is interested in it. The mistake managers often make is to assign the job to someone like Jim and *move on to something else,* failing to recognize that it is a yellow flag. Three weeks later, when the boss asks how that promotions project is coming along, he learns that very little has been accomplished. He wrings his hands and wonders why nothing ever gets done!

This executive is being unrealistic and shirking his own responsibility as a leader. His ultimate responsibility is not simply to parcel out work. It is to accomplish something. Why would he not follow through to make sure that Jim gets all the help he needs to succeed?

There are several possibilities. Some leaders believe in a sink-or-swim approach to managing. They may think of it as a test to see if Jim will rise to the occasion. There may even be some ego involved. The boss may feel that he himself never got any help when he was coming up through the ranks. Believe it or not, he may even feel a certain smug satisfaction if Jim fails, knowing that *he* would have succeeded. He may enjoy the feeling of superiority that he will have from having to bail out Jim.

Managers who have hidden agendas or whose intentions are far removed from the goal of productivity need to question their sincerity and motives. However, a more common reason managers don't follow through and help people with yellow flag assignments is that they don't realize that their people need the help. They don't know their strengths and weaknesses well enough.

Assigning a yellow flag may require more of a manager's cognitive and people skills than assigning other tasks. The goal in handling any yellow flag is to bring the person up to the capability needed to do it. If things go right, it will become a gold star for that person. If it is a one-time project, the manager will be taking his best shot at having it done well and on time despite the capability gap.

What is the remedy for making sure that yellow flag tasks are completed promptly and successfully? This is where a manager can show his resourcefulness:

- **Supervise the person closely.** The manager doesn't have to be a hovering threat, but she can work closely with the direct report in a supervisory capacity, offering suggestions and ideas to keep the assignment moving along. Before it's over, she may have to be coach, cheerleader, and a shoulder to lean on as well.

In fact, in some cases a manager actually may know how to do the task herself that she is assigning as a yellow flag to her direct report. If it is not a really urgent situation, her coaching provides a training experience. Obviously, it's a judgment call by the manager whether she should claim a project for herself to get it done fast or to provide a learning opportunity for the direct report. If the direct report acquires the skills needed, the next time the job comes along, it could well be a gold star that zips right through in record time.

- **Team the deficient person with someone else (or a group) who can fill in the gaps.** They both can benefit. It becomes a learning experience for the deficient person. It may be a gold star or a complementary yellow flag for the proficient team member who serves as trainer. Most important, the needed direction and information are brought to the task so that it gets done.

- **Bring in outside experts or formally train the deficient person.** In the bank example, a seminar may be available on the topic. Research time may be allowed. Instead of letting Jim fend for himself, he may thrive and end up becoming more valued as the resident authority on the subject.

Even when yellow flags are opportunities, it is important not to assign too many at one time. They could take up a disproportionate amount of the person's time and might be overwhelming.

3. ALLOWING BIG D (DISCIPLINE) ACTIVITIES TO SLOW THINGS DOWN

It is human nature to avoid work that is difficult, boring, or painful. Unfortunately, productivity in business depends as much on this kind of work getting done as the exciting, "glamorous" tasks. Probably more.

As a manager, you have to recognize the givens about the big D tasks. First, certain work can only be done by certain people. It can't be reassigned no matter how much it is disliked. An executive can't delegate a performance appraisal. A sales manager can't assign someone else to figure out her expense report. A boss shouldn't give another person the responsibility for hiring or firing someone.

Second, what each of these people can and frequently will do is try to avoid getting these tasks done. It's a natural impulse if the task is unpleasant. The trouble is, not only does the failure to act bog things down immediately, but the procrastination also has a ripple effect that creates additional logjams and backups. Big Ds gum up the works. Productivity slows down.

For example, what happens if a sales manager routinely avoids making out expense reports? It's a task she hates. So she puts it off as long as possible. This may mean that she is holding up information that is necessary for a variety of reports her department needs to file. Worse, her figures may end up not being included in timely documents that are used to make budget projections or other company decisions. It seems like a minor big D, but this ripple can have repercussions, especially if multiplied by the number of employees who have the same struggle. Procrastination on one big D task is hurting the company. Yet it may never be recognized as a problem.

Third, some people *do* need a nudge, a push, or something more substantial to get a big D task done. Even if they recognize its importance, they lack the drive to get started or to see it through to completion. What do you do? First, although big Ds are often unavoidable, make sure that you aren't turning one person's routine gold star task into a big D for someone else.

For instance, it could be this simple: The head of fleet rentals for a car leasing firm has a client that one of his salespeople, Biff, hates but another, Betty, likes. Why would he thoughtlessly send Biff to call on that person? He is creating a big D for Biff. It's not that Biff won't act professionally making the call, but he may procrastinate and have to be pushed and cajoled just to make the appointment. Meanwhile, the same task would be a gold star for Betty. Why jeopardize the client contact?

A variation on this is turning your own task into someone else's big D by needlessly delegating it. This is sometimes called "getting the monkey off your back." It's a philosophy that says that the way to get all your work done is to give it to someone else. It's real shortsighted thinking. Why delegate a task that will take 10 minutes to do if it will take your direct report hours or even days simply because he will gnash his teeth and stall and do everything else but get it done—until he just has to? So it is important not to create big Ds when it's not necessary because there will be enough necessary ones to go around.

Keep in mind that having big Ds is not the problem. What business doesn't have important things that have to be done that are tedious, boring, or just not liked?

The error for you as a manager is in not insisting the big Ds get done. As with yellow flags, you may not be able to assign a big D and walk away. Part of your job as someone who gets things accomplished is staying on top of those big Ds. The discipline that your direct reports must summon to get the task done may have to be matched by your own discipline to uphold work standards and follow up on the task.

For instance, Kathryn, an executive for a nationwide plastics manufacturer, is evaluating a number of employees for a new position. Before she makes her choice, though, she wants the latest performance appraisals of the candidates from several plant managers. One plant manager, Tim, does a great job, but writing formal evaluations of his direct reports is a big D for him. He puts it off. Or his procrastination could stem from not wanting to give an untruthful appraisal but also not wanting to lose the employee to a promotion. Whatever the case, Kathryn has always allowed Tim to turn in his appraisals months after the due date. Now she is paying for it. She doesn't want to pick someone from Tim's staff if that person's appraisal would be a problem. She needs that information. Tim's big D is creating a logjam for a number of other important decisions that must wait on him.

While this example is not an insurmountable problem, if enough big Ds are allowed to linger on and on, the collective drag on a department or entire company can be enormous.

If Kathryn could turn back the clock, here's what she could do: A few weeks before the appraisals are due, she could make it a point to *enlist Tim's commitment to the task*. She could *counsel him* on the importance of completing the appraisals not only for the company but also for the sake of his own people. She might serve as *coach* to gain his enthusiasm for doing this task that he doesn't enjoy. Some timely e-mail reminders might be helpful too as the deadline approaches. If it's a particularly important or complicated big D, she could even develop with Tim a formal *action plan*. But the message would have to come through clearly: *Get the thing done!*

Even the top executives of large corporations can be guilty of fumbling their own big Ds. For one thing, they often have more formidable big Ds than other people in their organizations. Some difficult decisions can only be made by the top people. In fact, in some organizations the only matters brought to a CEO or president of the company are the problems that cannot be solved at another level. Budget cuts, layoffs, promotions, and legal actions all apply.

Also, as people move up in their world, the definition of what kind of work they like changes. What was a challenge to do for the first 10 or 20 years can become drudgery. This doesn't mean that it isn't important. For instance, while the creation of a corporation's annual report can be carried out by various people, the top executives should still have a big hand in it. After all, it's the company's presentation of itself for all the world to see. But it's not likely to be exciting stuff to work on. The same can be said for representing the company at obligatory social functions.

Generally, a big D occurs when the perceived importance of the project and the affinity for doing it don't go together in a winning combination. This is why big Ds can pop up on a daily basis in rather mundane but significant ways. Returning phone calls and reading and responding to mail can feel like a bothersome grind for anyone. *Not* doing these activities can have a detrimental effect on productivity. Again, the principle is that a delay in responding to someone may hold up someone else's productivity, which in turn may affect still others.

4. MISSING GOLD STAR OPPORTUNITIES

Each of the other four errors involves some negative aspects of work assignments. They are all less-than-perfect combinations of our three variables—importance, capability, and enjoyment. This particular error involves the optimal tasks that have everything positive going for them—the gold stars.

Ideally, everyone's work should be a gold star. Most of the problems of productivity, morale, enthusiasm, drive, and so on would disappear if each task were ideal. Barring this possibility, doesn't it make sense as a manager to provide for as many gold stars as possible? Aren't gold stars the motivation for most people? Aren't they the definition of rewarding work? How can you arrange for them?

One answer was provided in discussing yellow flags and big Ds. By matching the right people with the right tasks, a manager can turn a potential yellow flag, big D, or even red flag for one person into a gold star for another. However, doing this means *knowing your people's capabilities and what they like to do*. It also may mean that when you assign work, you should look beyond each person's job slot, functional responsibilities, and the organization chart.

For example, Raymond heads up a nationwide appliance company whose assembly plant in Pittsburgh is having quality control problems. He needs to find out why. His organization chart says that a particular vice president, Stan, would be the correct person to send. Raymond knows, though, that while Stan understands the product thoroughly, he does not have the personality or mind-set for investigating, asking probing questions, and then holding people's feet to the fire if necessary to get things corrected.

So for Stan this assignment will be either a red flag or a big D. Chances are that Stan will return without solving the problem, and it will have to be confronted all over again. However, after giving it some thought, Raymond decides that he will pair Stan with Barbara, whose job title does not carry the authority that Stan's does but who has a good record for troubleshooting problems. Even though Barbara doesn't know much about appliance assembly, Stan certainly does. Now both people can concentrate on what they do best individually. In essence, Raymond has turned this task into two gold stars.

Here's another example that sometimes occurs in business. Let's say that the distribution center for a retail electronics firm needs to be moved. Typically, the current head of the distribution center is given the job of moving it. But why assume expertise at *running* an organization qualifies that person for *moving* that organization? Sure, he knows a lot about the facility. But this assignment probably will be a huge yellow or red flag.

The thoughtful leader would find someone who is an expert at moving a business, even if she has to go outside. Then the expert could confer with the head of the distribution center, whose role in the move now would be that of advisor. In fact, the distribution center's director might head up a team to recommend changes in the new distribution center—kind of a wish list for the move. This is a valuable contribution and a gold star for the head of the center.

Again, a key to arranging for work to become a gold star is to know your people well and to avoid the rigid thinking dictated by the organization chart. It demands that you not see assigning work as a series of narrow decisions. This confines your thinking. It keeps you from seeing how you might *structure* a project differently or slice it into a new configuration that uses people's talents and enthusiasms to their best advantage.

In the two examples just described, the manager applied creative thinking and avoided a knee-jerk response to assigning work. The goal is not to be neat and tidy or keep everyone in the little boxes we build for them in our minds. The goal is to get something done. Is it better to follow protocol and have quality control problems that continue month after month? Or could you get the thing taken care of within weeks by deploying people in the best possible way?

There's one other problem associated with gold stars that is important to discuss. One big reason a manager may pass up assigning gold stars is that he keeps the best assignments for himself.

Why would he do this? First of all, everyone needs his own gold stars. So it is not wrong for a manager on any level to keep some of these for himself. Another reason is that a project may require the global thinking of a manager before he divides up the work for direct reports.

For instance, because of a timely opportunity, a company may find itself having more floor space than it needs as part of a new lease agreement. How best to use the space? Before presenting this pleasant problem to all the department heads, the boss may want to study it herself to get a companywide perspective. This could change how she presents the assignment to her people.

So a manager has some good reasons for keeping gold stars. The test is, What is the motivation? A manager may hoard gold stars out of jealousy and insecurity. Perhaps, he feels threatened when a direct report handles an important job better than he would. Next time he decides to keep it for himself. Why make a hero out of someone who might take his job?

Only you can decide if you are keeping gold stars for yourself as a power issue or to protect your turf. Whatever the reason, over time the result will be the same. When employees feel that their boss is making his own job a paradise by keeping all the plum assignments and dishing out the "crumbs" to everyone else, they will approach their work a lot differently. The result can be lower productivity or the loss of quality employees who decide to look elsewhere for their own gold stars.

5. ASSIGNING RED FLAG ACTIVITIES

Red flag activities are perhaps the most detrimental to an organization. Here is vital work that needs to be done. Yet the manager who turns it into a red flag assignment virtually dooms it from the start. What is the likelihood that it will be done quickly or correctly if the people who carry it out aren't qualified and hate doing it? You can see that the future of a company that has too many red flags is in doubt.

Unlike yellow flags and big Ds, red flags always stem from a poor management decision. We know that many yellow flags are the result of an unavoidable competence gap, which can be overcome in time and are a training opportunity. Human nature makes big Ds difficult, but they too can be mastered. In fact, a vital, evolving organization will always have its share of yellow flags and big Ds. On the other hand, red flags are a dead end. An individual manager and the entire corporate culture should have zero tolerance for them. They just don't need to happen. Thus, when they pop up, they must be corrected immediately.

For example, Mary, a hospital administrator, has risen to her position because she combines so well her thorough knowledge of hospitals, medicine, and human resources. Her boss gives her the job of negotiating the contracts for the food services and self-service drink machine vendors at the hospital. She hates this task and is terrible at it. It is no surprise that contract talks always extend past their deadlines and rarely turn out to the hospital's advantage.

Another example: Ben, a merchandising manager for a chain of sportswear stores, is given inventory management responsibilities. While both tasks seem to be in the same ballpark, in this case they are not. Ben's entire orientation in his work is centered on fashion. This is what he is good at, and his love for it motivates him to excel. He has never been interested in the nuts and bolts of the business, including inventory control.

In both cases the boss is assigning tasks to the wrong people. For what reasons? They are very similar to the error a manager makes who needlessly creates yellow flags. He isn't thinking about the best match of people to tasks. Perhaps, in the case of

Mary, he is following the hospital's organization chart. Maybe her job description includes this. Or maybe he is just not thinking about what makes Mary tick. The same could be true for Ben's boss. He may be meeting his company's requirements for allocating personnel, but he sure isn't thinking about what makes Ben an excellent employee or how best to ensure that the inventory is handled well.

While the causes for making these errors can be similar to those that result in yellow flags, at least yellow flags have a good chance of being completed. People assigned them have a positive attitude and want to learn the skills needed to succeed. What chance is there for red flags when the people involved approach them with dread? The likely outcome is that the unfortunate employee will procrastinate, feel overwhelmed, panic, and, oh yes, fail miserably. In some cases a red flag can be motivation for leaving the company.

There is one other reason a manager would knowingly assign someone a red flag. He wants to punish the employee. Sometimes a black hole is assigned with the same motive, but in the case of a red flag, the task is *important*. He is using the job assignment to send a message or exert pressure on his direct report to fail or leave. It's the equivalent of sending someone to Siberia. By subverting the whole purpose of assigning work, the manager is jeopardizing his own future and the company's, to some extent, for a short-term purpose.

The remedy to a red flag is to reassign the task right away. At worst, make it someone's yellow flag or big D and provide the appropriate help or discipline.

These five errors comprise many of the problems managers have in assigning work. Using the task management model as a way of defining these errors allows you to see clearly the nature of the problems and what adjustments you should make for each.

DON'T BE PULLED OFF COURSE

This chapter began by stating that the main reason these errors occur is the lack of analysis of the work that managers assign and the people they assign to do it. So many decisions are made without forethought or planning.

Conflicting concerns and feelings also can cloud rational thinking and pull managers off course in making good management decisions. The result can lead to any of the five errors. Here is a summary of some of these influences on managers, all of which were touched on in explaining the errors. Are you allowing any of these to distort your assessment of people and the work you assign?

- Preoccupied with activities other than performance
- Feeling more comfortable assigning unimportant, familiar tasks than important but anxiety-provoking tasks
- Neglecting to differentiate tasks with regard to the importance, skills, or the emotional elements associated with them

- Having a theory X attitude about direct reports, that is, people don't like to work and won't take responsibility or commit to doing a good job (We will discuss this Q1 behavior in Chapter 6.)
- Fearing that direct reports may succeed and outshine you in getting important work done
- Reserving important tasks for yourself to increase your perceived power and visibility
- Supporting a corporate culture whose values place more importance on mere activity (being busy) than on getting results

A special situation may occur in which the five major errors are put aside in favor of getting a task accomplished promptly and completely. This situation occurs when a crisis hits a company. Chapter 5 explores crisis management and the lessons it teaches about focusing an entire organization's efforts.

CHAPTER 5

MANAGING IN A CRISIS MODE—WITHOUT THE CRISIS!

Next week there can't be any crisis. My schedule is already full.

Henry Kissinger,
former Secretary of State

Every day it seems that we learn about a prominent business or other organization being rocked by a crisis. A few examples remind us that crises develop quickly and that no business is immune:

> December 1994—A Virginia math professor alerts the Intel Corporation that its Pentium computer chip has a flaw. The defect shows up when certain sophisticated math functions are performed. IBM, a big Pentium customer, adds its voice to the concern and refuses to ship any more of its personal computers with Pentium chips. Eventually, Intel decides to give a free, flawless replacement chip to anyone requesting one. That covers 2.2 million chips in use.
>
> August 2000—Bridgestone/Firestone, Inc., decides to recall 6.5 million of its tires, many of them standard equipment on the Ford Explorer. The company takes the action after tread separation in their tires is linked to road accidents that have resulted in numerous deaths and injuries. The recall leads to the termination

of a 95-year business relationship with Ford. Besides the cost of the recall, Bridgestone suffers a $1 billion loss of income in the next fiscal year.

August 2000—A fake press release is picked up by several financial wire services on the Internet stating that Emulex Corporation's CEO has resigned and that the company is under investigation by the Securities and Exchange Commission. This causes the company's stock price to drop from $110 to $43 a share in minutes, resulting in a $2 billion loss in value. The company halts trading of the stock while the "fired" CEO appears on television to assure investors that the press release is a hoax. The quick and decisive actions work, and the stock slowly regains its value.

While most crises are not this severe, no one welcomes a crisis. Almost all emergencies, however, have at least one thing in common relevant to this book. A crisis can really drive an organization toward getting the right things done.

True, not all companies handle a crisis well. Some leaders panic and make bad decisions as a result. For them, the crisis can deliver a mortal blow. Time after time, however, organizations that normally are productive and operating at capacity are able to double or triple the amount of work they usually accomplish.

What happens during a crisis that elevates performance? What roadblocks that normally suppress such achievement are brushed aside? The goal of this chapter is to identify the reasons productivity rises so dramatically during a crisis and apply that knowledge to raising productivity during normal times when there is no emergency.

It should be emphasized, though, that this chapter is not about managing crises. No prescription exists for making the correct decisions in a crisis. Obviously, they are different for every emergency. Rather, this chapter will analyze the dynamics of crisis behavior and show why the task management model really comes to life in crisis circumstances.

Five fundamental behavioral changes occur during a crisis that help to account for the rise in performance:

1. **People focus on common goals.** This may be the common denominator for all crisis-driven behavior. Because the very existence of the company is often at stake, business as usual is abandoned. The routine internal conflicts over corporate goals or personal agendas that can hinder productivity are put aside. A crisis promotes teamwork. It unifies an organization to work toward accomplishing one goal—overcoming the crisis. Stated in terms of the model, a crisis forces everyone to focus on what's important. Everybody is expected to pitch in and help. With the possibility of imminent collapse, it is amazing how people get out of the basement and start working upstairs, doing meaningful tasks at least until the crisis is over.

2. **People display a refreshingly high degree of candor.** You know the problems a company can have when protocol, titles, deferential behavior, status issues, jealousy, office politics, egos, and general "CYA" behavior interfere with communicating solid information and advice. A full-blown crisis shoves all that aside. It is essential during a crisis that leaders have a steady flow of correct information, as well as quality ideas and opinions that are untainted. Realizing how high the stakes are, people will put aside the usual misgivings they may have about speaking up.

3. **The structural hierarchy of the organization is set aside.** Not entirely, of course. However, a crisis calls for answers—fast! When a tornado rips through a manufacturing plant, there's no time to worry about who are the "correct" people to rush to the scene. It's the people best able to deal with the disaster. When a restaurant chain suffers a food-poisoning incident, it welcomes help in dealing with this emergency from anyone in the organization competent to help regardless of job title or position.

4. **Cognitive skills are enhanced.** Part of the reason is physiologic. During a crisis, we experience an increase in adrenaline. We are energized. Our senses sharpen. Because we have a heightened awareness of what's going on around us, we take in more information.

We also deliberately program our minds to pay better attention, tuning in to what will help us.

5. **Leaders assign tasks more effectively.** This is the logical culmination of the previous points. Because of the urgency and high stakes, leaders *do* assign tasks more effectively in a crisis. So much more rides on each decision. And they are aided by individuals stepping up and volunteering for tasks that they know they can get done.

Now let's review a classic case to illustrate these and other crisis behaviors in action.

CRISIS RESPONSE TO A BITTER PILL

On the business crisis meter, the Tylenol poisonings that took place in 1982 registered a 10. Seven people in the Chicago area died from poisoning after taking Extra-Strength Tylenol laced with cyanide. The brand seemed doomed.

James E. Burke, the chairman of Johnson & Johnson (J&J), the parent company of the drug's manufacturer, took steps that are a textbook case of how to manage a crisis. He immediately organized investigative teams to find out exactly what happened. An information center was set up where managers worked telephone banks and pulled together the story while it developed. As events unfolded, Burke transferred running the company to other executives while he took full charge of the crisis.

J&J decided to pull all 31 million bottles of Tylenol from store shelves nationwide at a cost of $100 million. It sent 500,000 mailgrams to doctors, hospitals, and distributors announcing the recall.

High marks have been given to J&J for its candor in informing the public about its actions and not trying to manage the news. Twenty-five public relations staff members were assigned to handle the huge communications problem of dealing with the media, clients, health authorities, law enforcement, and the public. At no time did these groups feel that corporate leaders were stonewalling or hiding information.

As weeks went by, J&J entered the latter stages of what is now the classic pattern of crisis management: Identify the problem, control it, fix it, and do whatever it takes so that it never happens again.

J&J also decided to try to save the brand. The new tamperproof Tylenol was on store shelves just 10 weeks after the crisis began. Over 2000 sales reps made a million telephone calls to physicians and pharmacists to spread the word. By the following April, the pain reliever, which had dipped to just 4 percent of the market, had climbed back to 24 percent.

The company's leaders were able to save Tylenol by concentrating their efforts and mobilizing quickly. No one knew a crisis was coming, but as often happens in a crisis, J&J figured out very quickly how to get the right things done.

ON THEIR BEST BEHAVIOR

There is no doubt that the performance of the leaders and everyone else at J&J was elevated during the Tylenol crisis. What were the common elements of crisis behavior that are useful lessons to apply to raising productivity when there is no crisis?

PEOPLE CONCENTRATE ON GETTING IMPORTANT THINGS DONE

From the chairman on down at J&J, the corporation's entire population was keenly aware of their common goal. During the crisis, their reason for going to work every day had real meaning and purpose.

It takes constant effort over a period of time for a company to convey its vision and mission to employees during normal times. It is astounding how in a crisis the goal is crystallized for everyone almost instantly. Imagine what could be accomplished by establishing that kind of focus all the time.

CANDOR IS RAISED SIGNIFICANTLY

It was important for J&J to let the world know what it was doing to solve the crisis. A cover-up would have broken faith with a public relying on the safety of over-the-counter medications.

Just as important, in order to understand and investigate quickly exactly what it was dealing with, the leadership of J&J made sure that everyone internally was staying informed. A command post was set up to get a handle on the facts, dispel rumors, and disseminate information. Candor also told them what they had to do to regain the confidence of the public. While it was a terrible blow to absorb, if these leaders had not recognized the truth of where they stood and pulled their entire product off the shelves, Tylenol as a brand probably would have folded.

The more candor a manager can count on in the workplace every day, the better equipped she will be at determining what work is important and the right people to do it.

HIERARCHICAL STRUCTURES FADE

The chairman of J&J turned over the day-to-day operations of his company to other executives while he concentrated on managing the crisis. This is typical behavior up and down the line in an emergency. Leaders recognize that solving the crisis takes precedence over following the organization chart.

CROSS-FUNCTIONAL COOPERATION OCCURS SPONTANEOUSLY

In the Tylenol case, the goal took precedence over protocol and "going through channels." Particularly while attempting to solve the crime, numerous departments and agencies that normally would have squabbled over jurisdictional matters worked together to share information and coordinate their efforts.

Surprisingly, a crisis often has this effect. People who thought they couldn't or wouldn't work together find themselves cooperating. What would happen within an organization after a crisis if this kind of cooperation simply continued?

IDEAS ARE GENERATED QUICKLY

Everyone recognizes that the deadline in a crisis is ASAP. The adrenaline flows. People push themselves to concentrate and put their creative thinking into overdrive. The good ideas happen—the bad ones are discarded immediately.

If many more ideas are produced by a crisis than would be normally, wouldn't it be great to trigger that kind of creative energy at other times?

PEOPLE ARE MORE OPEN TO INPUT FROM OTHERS

Just as entire departments and organizations work together more smoothly during a crisis, individually, people put their differences and status concerns aside for the common good. Worrying about who will get credit often takes a back seat.

PEOPLE ARE MORE WILLING TO TRY OUT NEW IDEAS

Perhaps tamperproof packaging was a good idea before the Tylenol deaths. However, there was no perceived need for it until the poisonings. Not only did Tylenol change its packaging, so did the rest of the industry, as mandated by new regulations. A crisis cries out for solutions. People who have been harboring good ideas with no one to champion them suddenly may find themselves willing to stick their necks out for a greater good. Think how innovative a company would be that could develop the same encouraging environment for new ideas all the time.

HIDDEN POTENTIAL EMERGES IN PEOPLE

This is similar to the previous point. Who knew that that person in public relations could turn around a news release so fast? Who knew that the person pressed into service to talk to clients had such great people skills? The executive who was forced to make corporate decisions while the J&J chairman was tied up with the crisis may have discovered that he had leadership capabilities he wasn't aware of before.

If it takes a crisis to bring out hidden potential, what if a company worked to find that same potential among its workforce as part of its everyday operations? Without burdening the payroll, it could increase its capabilities simply by recognizing and developing people's potential as an ongoing activity.

PEOPLE ARE LIBERATED FROM THE BARRIERS TO PERFORMANCE IMPROVEMENT

One such barrier is the habitual way people deal with each other and their bosses. Many people don't want to rock the boat at work. They smooth over problems and don't speak their minds about making improvements.

The gravity of a crisis can change these "rules of the game." People decide that because of the crisis, their concerns will matter and their voices will be heard. Thus there is more communication *upward* in an organization during a crisis. By speaking out, employees are able to remove many barriers to performance improvement. If this kind of fresh start brought on by the crisis could occur for noncrisis goals, how much more productive would people be?

PEOPLE SPONTANEOUSLY REACH GREAT HEIGHTS OF PERFORMANCE WITHOUT EXTENSIVE MANAGEMENT PLANNING

Not everyone does this, of course, but almost any crisis produces heroes that surprise everyone. This phenomenon is a result of people's heightened awareness and vigilance, as well as increased candor. The sense of openness and a willingness to experiment encourage people to step into the breech and make a contribution.

CRISIS MENTALITY

Now let's examine briefly several other examples to show how crisis behavior can cut through the turmoil of events to get the right things done.

THE MANAGERS OF OCTOBER

You probably don't think of government as an organization that is overworked or operating at high efficiency. However, in a crisis, even this leviathan can be awakened from business as usual to get enormous amounts of work done quickly.

History shows that there was no more dangerous confrontation during the Cold War than the Cuban missile crisis. Thus, when President John F. Kennedy was informed that offensive missiles were being erected in Cuba under the direction of the Soviet Union, he and his staff went into crisis mode.

The nation was fortunate in some ways that the President had previously endured a catastrophic executive decision that contrasted sharply with his behavior during the Cuban missile crisis. Kennedy had authorized the Bay of Pigs invasion in April 1961, and it was a complete debacle. Kennedy felt that he was misinformed by the CIA and military leaders about the project's chances for success. Shortly after landing in Cuba, hundreds of Cuban exiles were killed, and 1200 were captured by Fidel Castro's army.

Important to this discussion, Kennedy had an advisory group that on paper should have supplied him with enough good information to make a rational, cognitive decision. However, at the first meeting, Kennedy himself effectively closed off any meaningful dissent by stating openly his strong approval of the plan.

Because this was not a crisis atmosphere, the various cabinet members and advisors readily deferred to the President. His status weighed so heavily on this newly organized committee that few were willing to speak out against the plan.

By not going through the important search for complete information, Kennedy as manager failed in his assessment of what was important. He cut himself off from the candor needed to stimulate a true evaluation of what historians consider a doomed venture.

How did a crisis atmosphere change things? Eighteen months later when approximately the same group met to consider how to respond to the Cuban missile threat, the dynamics were much different. The President had been a fast learner. In conducting this new cognitive search, he withheld his own opinion. He made certain that a full discussion of options took place and encouraged dissent.

The crisis also fostered a sense of urgency that the Bay of Pigs may not have. Typically, a presidential advisory group brings to the table more protective self-interest than exists in most other organizations. However, this group of 14 was able to get things done because it had the advantage of crisis behavior that cuts through the usual barriers. All members focused on the gravity of their mission and readily cooperated with each other. Ideas flowed freely and quickly.

The committee developed six possible courses of action. Kennedy himself had to make the final decision, but candor made it possible for him to choose from a full array of options. He chose the naval blockade of Soviet delivery ships as a limited action, allowing negotiating room for both sides. Of course, that set up the climax of the crisis when Soviet ships turned away from confrontation at sea. An agreement was soon worked out calling for dismantling the missiles.

Thus in 13 days a group of government officials became energized, worked quickly, and achieved results because a crisis forced them to focus on what was important.

A 9/11 SUCCESS STORY

You are aware of the scores of extraordinary stories surrounding the 9/11 attack on the World Trade Center towers. The remarkable efforts of firefighters, police, and rescue workers have been recounted many times. So many other individuals and organizations demonstrated the outstanding performances that a crisis can generate. Do you recall, for instance, that in less than 3 hours after the first attack, the Federal Aviation Administration succeeded in landing all 4600 planes flying over the continental United States? Officials had never planned for this effort, much less rehearsed it, but the crisis focused everyone involved on the goal—halt all flying immediately.

In another behind-the-scenes performance, Verizon Communications met the challenge of a related crisis when the New York Stock Exchange's communications system was knocked out on 9/11. Many of its connections to member firms and the markets were severed because the nearby Verizon switching facility was damaged. Verizon supplied 80 percent of the phone lines to the NYSE.

Located next to the World Trade Center complex, Verizon's telecom nerve center normally housed 1737 employees. Service was knocked out by severed cables, a loss of power, and generators flooded by water from broken water mains. Equipment was covered in ash. This made the prospect doubtful for restoring even a part of the system very quickly.

Yet that is exactly what federal and local officials wanted. They viewed the reopening of the NYSE as a symbol to the world of the nation's resilience. So the pressure was on for the NYSE to reopen the Monday following the attack—four working days later! Most thought it impossible.

Still stunned by the World Trade Center collapse, Verizon's people organized into teams that attacked the many facets of the huge problem. The software needed to run the system could not be accessed in the damaged building. Duplicate software was tracked down from 10 years earlier when the system had first been set up. Thousands of new telephone lines were installed for brokerage firms that had to relocate away from the World Trade Center. These were supplemented by mobile wireless telephone transmitters. Verizon also added 24 high-speed data links in the area.

The weekend before the Monday morning deadline was frantic. The company felt overwhelmed by the complexity of the task. However, Verizon took advantage of its crisis mentality to get things done. It focused on one goal—the stock market had to reopen on Monday morning. The usual hierarchy was set aside in favor of an organizational structure whose only goal was to accomplish the steps needed to succeed. You can bet that when tasks were assigned, no one was working below the line.

Furthermore, people stepped up and worked smarter, applying all their knowledge to solve numerous problems under deadline pressure. It wasn't until 5 A.M. Monday that Verizon had the network ready to go. When the bell sounded at the NYSE, the financial markets were back in business!

LESSONS LOST

Ironically, once it's over, there's often very little follow-up to determine why the organization and its members behaved so differently during the crisis. Specifically

- **Leaders typically do not critique why extraordinary performances occurred.**
- **They accept it when the people involved in the crisis return to their normal, habitual ways of doing things.** If there is one change in behavior as a manager that the task management model is trying to encourage, it is *not* to accept the status quo as a given. Why assume that the output of a department or a whole company must be locked in at a certain level?
- **They rationalize that the crisis has nothing to teach them.** Rather than learning lessons to apply in the future, leaders may view the crisis as simply bad luck and want to move on. What happened may be seen as an embarrassment or a weakness of the existing leadership. Even when the crisis is the result of a natural disaster or sabotage, leaders may question their preparedness and feel guilty. Finger pointing can occur that asks, "Why didn't you see this coming?" "Who wasn't on the ball and let this happen?"
- **They overlook the profound significance of what the crisis revealed.** The crisis is not seen as an opportunity. The remarkable effort and the fact that for a while everyone was out of the basement working on things that really mattered are lauded as singular events. The principles behind them are missed. Life goes on.

LESSONS FOUND

You don't have to make the same mistake. You can use as a guide the positive behaviors that are exhibited so strikingly during a crisis and interpret them in the now-familiar terms of the task management model:

- **Stop doing all tasks that are below the line** (**in black hole territory**). It would be ludicrous to ask your people to do unnecessary tasks, whether they like them or not, when a crisis threatens the company. Does it make any more sense for time and energy to be spent on these activities when there isn't a crisis?

- **Determine what is *important* to get done.** It's the first order of business in a crisis. It should be a manager's first order of business every day. Take nothing for granted. Establish an atmosphere of candor to help find out.

- **Determine who is *capable* of getting each task done.** Anyone heading up the response to a crisis will tell you that it is crucial to choose people for critical tasks who are most likely to follow through and succeed. There may be no second chances. As a manager, you should bring the same sense of precision to assigning work every day.

- **Determine who will *enjoy* or dislike the tasks that need to be done.** Granted, during a crisis, no leader delegating a task really cares if the person likes it or not. In fact, many tasks in a crisis by definition are big Ds. Yet, even then, wise leaders grasp that some people will enjoy particular tasks more than others and will put more into them.

- **Violate the organization chart, if necessary, to turn as many jobs as possible into gold stars.** Managers in a crisis give little thought to whether it's okay to pass over a third vice president for a task because his feelings might be hurt. In an emergency, leaders' minds race ahead to who they think will do the best job.

  If you feel continually thwarted trying to match the best person to a task, it's time to question the organization chart. It should not be dictating how work is assigned but reflect the best way for work to flow.

  Of course, during normal times you might pay a price for ignoring your organization's structure. While you shouldn't jeopardize your job, you may be able to work around the chart in a judicious way. And it certainly makes sense to try to change the structure if it hurts productivity.

- **Coach for commitment, enthusiasm, and benefits for achieving big D tasks.** As mentioned earlier, many tasks during a crisis are big Ds. Fortunately, most people want to help save the day, and the benefits of working toward the greater goal are clear. So wise leaders tap into their employees' enthusiasm and pride of accomplishment.

A crisis teaches us, therefore, to find the motivation and commitment in people to deal with big Ds. You may need to coach employees to understand the benefits when assigning big Ds that are part of everyday work. Look at what happens, though, when this occurs during a crisis. People really do reach down and come through!

- **Supervise, support, provide information, and encourage building *complementary skills* throughout teams for yellow flag tasks.** During a crisis, people are often asked to carry out tasks for which they are not trained and have no experience. They have to learn fast and work effectively if they are going to be useful. It is amazing how much people can absorb and how fast they can get up to speed in this situation.

  One way the learning curve is accelerated in a crisis is by matching up people with complementary skills. A typical team often includes members with experience, those with training but no experience, those with only textbook knowledge, and finally, raw volunteers. When properly supervised and supported with help and information, they can share their skills and work together effectively.

  As a focused leader, you can use the same principles in assigning yellow flag tasks. Supervise closely, make sure direct reports are fully informed, and create teams for learning where the skills of the members complement each other.

- **Reassign red flags to make them gold star, big D, or yellow flag tasks.** The worst thing in a crisis is for people to be wasting time on red flags. Fortunately, leaders in an emergency are usually focused enough to avoid assigning them, and importantly, individuals will not accept them. Leaders may not be able to turn a red flag into someone else's gold star, but at least the crisis tasks will become big Ds or yellow flags, which can be handled and accomplished in ways we've explained.

SUSTAINING THE CRISIS MENTALITY

Perhaps at this point you are skeptical about whether it's possible to motivate employees to perform every day as they would in an emergency. Can you really substitute a corporate goal and get people to work the way they would when faced with product sabotage, terrorism, or the threat of nuclear war?

Not likely. However, leadership in a crisis serves as a paradigm for the kind of focused decision making the task management model helps you to make. The object is not to produce crisis-level stress, which would just lead to burnout. It's to show how a crisis can motivate to get the right things done.

The bottom-line message is this: During a crisis, very few, if any, of the errors occur that were highlighted in Chapter 4. While surely not the only factor, this is a key reason productivity in a crisis rises to such a high degree. Every day in the normal course of business when there's no crisis, avoiding these five errors as often as possible will lead to higher productivity.

We said in Chapter 2 that we wanted to go beyond style in order to present a more practical and usable system for getting more accomplished. Now it's time to revisit style in Chapter 6. What style on the job do you envision as being most effective for motivating your people?

CHAPTER 6

BACK IN STYLE AGAIN

Style is the perfection of a point of view.

Richard Eberhart,
American writer

Cheerleader	Glad-hander	Yes man
Tyrant	Pushover	Advisor
Coach	Teacher	Wimp
Taskmaster	S.O.B. or bitch	Role model
Cold fish	Leader	Suck-up
Buddy	Clueless	Empty suit
Mentor	Brown nose	Hero

This is a list of some typical labels people use to characterize the behavioral style of their bosses. Perhaps you have described a boss using one of these terms yourself. Perhaps your own direct reports would apply some of them to you. Only the positive ones, of course.

So far the discussion of the task management model has purposely avoided referring to individual style as a factor in applying management decisions. That's because a stated premise of this book is that while your managerial style matters, it will not make smart, sensible decisions for you about what is important or how to assign work. In the end, your style alone will not get the right things done.

For that, the model is a logical discipline for analyzing your decision making. It compels you to step back from personality issues to identify what is essential for making sound judgments. It also provides a dependable rationale for making assignments. In essence, the model is independent of style.

However, in this chapter style reenters the picture. Why now? At this point you are familiar with the cognitive process that task management employs. Yet, in the real world, a manager is not simply a human computer that prints out decisions after hitting the "Think" button. *How* you behave as a person and *how* you deal with people—that is, your style on the job—serve as the context and environment for your decisions.

While the labels listed at the beginning of this chapter are simplifications, it is safe to say that a direct report's response to her boss will vary depending on how she perceives him, for instance, as a "role model," a "tyrant," or a "wimp." Thus style will play a role in putting task management into practice.

For example, we have emphasized the importance of knowing your people to better understand and evaluate their capabilities. It is reasonable to think that one particular managerial style will be more effective than another in connecting with people.

We said that a high degree of candor in the workplace is a real advantage for a focused manager. What behavior on your part, then, is most apt to encourage your employees to be totally candid in dealing with you?

Or suppose that you are faced with tough decisions about eliminating black hole activities. This could mean reassigning people to new tasks. They may have to learn new, relevant skills in order to refocus on upstairs activities. Isn't it safe to assume that the approach you choose in gaining employees' commitment to change will have a substantial effect on how hard they try to succeed?

The question then becomes, Is there a particular style that best facilitates making task management decisions? From decades of research, we have been able to identify a particular set of behaviors that constitutes a style that will serve you best.

A MODEL OF THE FOUR BEHAVIORAL STYLES

To understand the style we recommend, it is necessary to sort out the wide variety of behavioral styles that managers display on the job. We employ a grid similar to the task management model. It is one we have used to help thousands of executives gain insight about their employees and themselves. Its validity has been substantiated over the 45 years it has been applied in the corporate world.*

It is simpler than the task management model because it is made up of just two dimensions:

*Psychological Associates, a human resources development organization, has been employing the model described in this chapter in people skills seminars and training programs for thousands of businesspeople worldwide. For more information about the model, refer to *Leadership Through People Skills*, by R. E. Lefton and V. R. Buzzotta (New York: McGraw-Hill, 2004.)

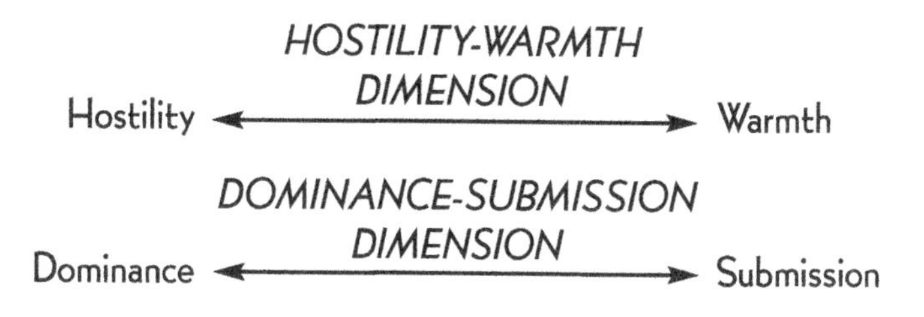

To understand the interplay among these qualities, let's first define what they mean:

> **Warmth.** A high regard for people; an awareness, sensitivity, and responsiveness to the needs, ideas, and feelings of others.
>
> **Hostility.** Lack of regard for people; a lack of awareness, sensitivity, and responsiveness to the needs, ideas, and feelings of others.
>
> **Dominance.** Taking charge or control; being forceful, assertive, and guiding.
>
> **Submission.** Relinquishing control; being passive and unassertive and allowing others to take charge.

The *hostility-warmth dimension* measures regard for people along a continuum from extreme hostility to extreme warmth. The *dominance-submission dimension* gauges how dominating a person is, also along a continuum.

These dimensions can be represented as two intersecting lines that define four areas, or quadrants. The quadrants correspond to four distinct behavioral styles, designated Q1 through Q4. Let's look at each as a way of characterizing how a manager approaches his job and his people.

MANAGEMENT BEHAVIOR STYLES

Dominance

Q1 = Tell and Do

Communication
One way
Decisions
"One alone"
Motivation
Uses fear, threats, coercion
Conflict Management
Suppresses conflict
Impact on People
Minimal development, alienation, burn-out

Q4 = Challenge and Involve

Communication
Two way, open and candid
Decisions
Maximum input; intense deliberation
Motivation
Builds understanding and commitment to goals
Conflict Management
Encourages divergent points of view; creative solutions
Impact on People
Maximum development; enlists full skill and potential

Hostility ← → **Warmth**

Q2 = Avoid and Abdicate

Communication
Avoidance; vague, ambiguous
Decisions
Safe; protects status quo; no input
Motivation
Uninvolved; little direction
Conflict Management
Avoidance; plays it safe
Impact on People
Low achievement; frustration, apathy

Q3 = Pacify and Socialize "Let's be pals."

Communication
Rarely candid; superficial, glosses over disagreement
Decisions
Seeks acceptance and what is popular
Motivation
Tries to please; no challenge
Conflict Management
Smooths over; easily compromises or gives in
Impact on People
Confusion; little development

Submission

Q1 HOSTILE-DOMINANT

This style combines a negative attitude about people with controlling, dominating behavior. The manager who behaves in a Q1 manner is a strong authoritarian, driven by a need to control and to prop up his self-esteem. Because maintaining his power is so important, he has a constant need to be recognized. He certainly is not interested in sharing power. Since he sees others as a threat to his turf, he must aggressively guard what is his.

We can further understand the Q1 style (and the other three styles as well) by looking at how it affects typical skills that managers must employ on the job:

Working with people. Because the Q1-style manager has a low regard for people, he assumes that his direct reports are incompetent, lazy, and stupid. He knows in advance that the work he assigns will have to be watched and controlled. Thus he responds in one of two ways: If he delegates at all, the Q1-style manager is apt to assign tasks below people's ability levels, believing he himself is the only one trustworthy enough to get things done correctly. Or this lack of trust reveals itself in the need to micromanage his direct reports, attempting to ensure that their assignments will turn out exactly the way he wants.

Making decisions. The Q1-style manager makes all the important decisions by himself. Consulting with others or soliciting advice is seen as a waste of time. It opens the door to sharing authority and control.

Communication. Communication is simple for a Q1-style manager. He talks; you listen. Why would someone with such a low opinion of people be interested in what others have to say? Input from people who work for a Q1-style manager is minimal.

Conflict management. Since the Q1-style manager discounts people, conflict in the workplace isn't resolved. It is simply squelched. Only one point of view matters. For this reason, tension is usually high because hostility and anger are generated from unresolved issues. This can have a drastic effect on morale as well.

Gaining people's understanding and commitment. The Q1-style manager uses power to require employees to fall into lockstep with his vision and goals. Intimidation and threats replace understanding and commitment. This manager strives for capitulation instead of commitment. Many employees burn out under Q1-style managers, whereas others simply quit because no attempt has been made to secure their loyalty or trust.

The Impact of Q1 Behavior on People Management

Because a Q1-style manager is so unconnected to people, he assigns work poorly. He cuts off his potential for matching the capabilities of his people to the job by not taking advantage of the intellectual resources of others. His direct reports are given little help with red or yellow flags. He imposes a sink-or-swim attitude. When assigning big Ds, he neither counsels nor attempts to develop understanding and commitment.

A Q1-style manager also hoards gold star assignments to get all the glory. Even if he reluctantly parcels one out, he will micromanage that person rather than letting her excel on her own.

Q2 HOSTILE-SUBMISSIVE

Q2-style behavior is marked by apathy and a very superficial involvement with people. While Q1 behavior means cracking the whip, the Q2-style manager is not concerned with productivity. Her major concern is her own security and well-being. Thus she protects the status quo. She tends to be cautious and keeps her distance when dealing with people. As someone described the Q2, "She has been handed a managerial sword but spends most of her time trying to put it back in her scabbard."

Working with people. The Q2-style manager is wary, aloof, and guarded. She does not view her role as leading, stimulating, or guiding employees. While Q1 hostility may translate into browbeating others, the Q2-style manager is apathetic. By keeping her distance, she is apt to let people do what they want. Thus she provides little guidance or help for becoming more capable.

Making decisions. The Q2-style manager wants to keep decision making safe and negligible. She involves others only superficially in the process because she isn't comfortable with contention and conflict. Consequently, very few bold or innovative ideas emerge. In making assignments, rather than concentrate on evaluating skills and motivation, she clings to a rote system of assigning people. She may even make an assignment on the basis of whoever happened to wander by her desk at that moment.

Communication. Instead of two-way or even one-way communication, the Q2-style manager fosters *no-way* communication. Direct reports are lucky to have any interaction at all, much less to get input about assignments or receive feedback about performance. When a Q2-style manager does communicate, she is usually vague, ambiguous, and/or neutral.

Conflict management. As you might expect, the Q2 style of playing it safe and opting for security results in avoidance of conflict. By withdrawing from involvement, the Q2-style manager simply avoids handling problems.

Gaining people's understanding and commitment. Because the Q2-style manager avoids interaction, she does little to rally people or enlist their resources on behalf of her company. She doesn't explain or get others involved in her decisions. She doesn't coordinate goals among her people. They are generally left to their own devices. Consequently, she generates little understanding, passion, or commitment.

The Impact of Q2 Behavior on People Management

It isn't difficult to predict. A Q2-style manager does what is safe, not what is important. She strives for sameness from day to day and year to year. Because she doesn't connect with people or know them well, she does not take a hand in enabling direct reports to succeed when faced with yellow flag, big D, or even red flag tasks.

Her lack of commitment or involvement and her passivity also mean that a Q2-style manager will tolerate a lot of black hole activity. She easily accepts people working in the basement.

Q3 WARM-SUBMISSIVE

Q3-style management is marked by a continuous need to be accepted and liked by others. Getting along with people could be a real plus to help inspire and motivate. However, the Q3-style manager is far more concerned with making popular decisions than with achieving results. This manager is willing to compromise quickly and won't take a stand for long if it ruffles someone's feathers.

Working with people. The Q3-style manager believes that pleasing people is more important than challenging them. Therefore, he sets very broad, easily achievable goals that can be revised continually to accommodate people. His need to please keeps him from holding them accountable. He thinks that by letting direct reports set their own agendas, they will reach high levels of productivity. However, his passivity keeps him from challenging them to reach high standards.

Making decisions. Instead of making decisions in terms of what will drive the business and increase productivity, the Q3-style manager asks what will be the most popular action. Q3 behavior means letting people vote a lot, not as a way of being inclusive, but to dodge responsibility for making unpopular choices.

Communication. It is difficult to have a candid, balanced dialogue with someone who exhibits Q3 behavior. He only wants to talk about what is pleasant and acceptable. He doesn't bring up bad news and will change the subject to avoid disagreement. In essence, the Q3-style manager is only engaging in partial communication.

Conflict management. What conflict? The Q3-style manager's goal is to smooth over conflict. If that doesn't work, rather than use conflict as the springboard for fresh ideas or new solutions, he will reach for a hasty compromise or give in altogether.

Gaining people's understanding and commitment. By not engaging in candid discussions, the Q3-style manager squanders the opportunity to give direct reports a full understanding of their roles in the organization. After all, there's never a reality check as a basis for such an understanding. Also, by not pushing for commitment, the Q3-style manager develops minimal passion in people.

The Impact of Q3 Behavior on People Management

It will have quite an adverse effect. The driving force is for doing what is popular, not for getting the right things done. In fact, Q3 behavior makes it hard to boost employees' capabilities because there's no honest evaluation. Everyone's performance is great.

More specifically, the Q3 environment is a breeding ground for black holes. There's no accountability when people are performing irrelevant tasks. If the Q3-style manager can keep people happy, he's doing his job.

Q4 WARM-DOMINANT

The regard the Q4-style manager shows for people motivates her to stimulate involvement and connect with others. Her willingness to be active and decisive compels her to challenge employees and set high standards. This is a powerful combination. It allows the Q4-style manager to create the best conditions for identifying what is important and making the right assignments.

The Q4-style manager seeks autonomy and growth. She knows that her objective is to increase productivity and drives to reach the bottom-line goals of her organization. She accomplishes this by using her involved relationship with her people to (1) guide them, (2) assist them in understanding their decisions and goals, and (3) draw on the intellectual capital they represent and thus increase their productivity.

The manager using the Q4 style is able to "unleash" involvement because she takes the time to get people on board and in synch with immediate and long-term goals. She vigorously includes them in solving problems. She seeks input, knowing that by soliciting a variety of opinions and viewpoints, her final decision will be more informed. This is what teamwork is all about—drawing on the resourcefulness and strengths of individuals to generate ideas and solutions far superior to those any one individual would have produced on his own.

Working with people. The Q4-style manager is optimistic and upbeat about people. She believes that they will work hard when they are involved and understand. This reflects a respect for people that is lacking in the other styles identified. While Q1-style managers exploit people, Q4-style managers exploit the *intellectual resources* of people.

Making decisions. The Q4-style manager does not make decisions out of insecurity. Her decisions are not about what is popular or what is safe but what is *best*. She asks, "Will this decision drive our business?" And she doesn't go it alone. The decisions she makes draw on the resources of her people.

Communication. Involving people and challenging them will not work without open, candid, two-way communication. The Q4-style manager promotes engaging dialogue.

Conflict management. Rather than viewing conflict as a threat or a failure, the Q4-style manager believes that conflict can be an opportunity, a way to reach a positive outcome. Q1-style managers squelch conflict. Q2- and Q3-style managers avoid it one way or another. The Q4-style manager invites a clash of ideas because she feels that disagreements can be the catalyst to better decisions and more creative solutions.

Gaining people's understanding and commitment. This is a top priority for a Q4-style manager. She believes that by involving her people, she can get them to understand the goals she is trying to reach. From that understanding she can achieve their commitment to pursue those goals and work hard to attain them.

The Impact of Q4 Behavior on People Management

The Q4-style manager facilitates all the priorities of the three dimensions in the task management model. Her openness, candor, and ability to connect with people allow her to get solid information through two-way communication. This helps her to zero in on what is important and which people should handle an assignment.

A Q4-style manager gets more done because she is willing to put the tough issues on the table. She has the confidence to confront people in a constructive way. She is willing to engage in a spirited dialogue that deals with problems, sorts them out, and builds solutions. This allows the organization to move forward rather than getting bogged down by the same old barriers.

Because the Q4-style manager establishes direction and provides autonomy, she frequently and generously assigns gold stars and lets people alone to excel at them. She knows that when she assigns a big D, her direct report will not like it. However, because she also knows the particular person well, she can counsel him effectively and appeal to him in an individual way. She also understands the risks of assigning yellow flags, but her concern for and knowledge of the people involved will give her insights about what to do to inspire, educate, and bring people up to the skill levels needed. She also believes in teamwork to accomplish this.

Q4 IS YOUR BEST OPPORTUNITY

From this overview of the four management styles it is obvious that we advocate Q4 behavior as the most beneficial for practicing task management. The Q4 style gives you your best opportunity to carry out your task assessments effectively. The chart at the end of this chapter compares the four styles in relation to several task management concerns.

Keep in mind, though, that the descriptions of the four styles are generalizations. For instance, no one in real life outside of a Dickens novel is a pure Q1. The same goes for the other quadrants. All of us exhibit a combination of all four behaviors on the job, and we may act differently from moment to moment.

The idea is to recognize trends and tendencies. You shouldn't feel that if you do not have a perfect Q4 style, you can't practice good task management. Being more Q4 simply paves the way for applying the task management model more effectively. For instance, you know that these Q4 characteristics will be valuable to adopt whether or not you are the model of Q4 behavior all the time:

- Generating candor
- Promoting collaboration
- Increasing involvement and connecting with people
- Constantly communicating your department's and organization's goals, mission, vision, values, and plan

- Emphasizing feedback
- Setting high standards
- Articulating clear goals and expectations

Can you actually change your style to become more Q4? While your behavioral style may reflect your personality to some degree, it is not the same thing as your personality. We have found over the years that people benefit greatly from analyzing their style to get fresh insights about themselves and what their behavior says to others. People can change their behavior by becoming more aware and learning behavior skills. We feel that it is possible to move away from the negatives of the Q1, Q2, and Q3 styles and begin behaving in a new way.

FROM MANAGEMENT TO LEADERSHIP

When does a successful Q4 management style become successful leadership? Are they the same thing?

A lot has been written in recent years about leadership and what makes an effective leader. Some take a practical approach, whereas others make leadership seem an almost magical quality. Napoleon Bonaparte, one of history's great leaders, offered an interesting definition: "A leader is a dealer in hope." There's no question that many leaders succeed, at least in the short run, by drawing on a heavy dose of personal magnetism.

When businesspeople discuss leadership, their concern is with those qualities leaders have to set a course for where they want to take their organizations and how they marshal the efforts of their people to get there. Successful corporate leaders define the vision, mission, values, and goals of their companies in order to take a vigorous role in leading their workforce. They also devise a plan of action for achieving those goals.

We believe that applying the task management model in a Q4 way lays a strong foundation for successful leadership. To substantiate this idea, let's look at a comprehensive definition of the term as applied in business. It is a composite of the common elements most frequently mentioned in business literature:

> Leadership is a process of creating a vision, communicating it, influencing others to carry it out, and setting an example that inspires and directs the actions of others in accord with the leader's purpose or the shared purpose of all.

This is quite a mouthful, but even as a textbook definition, it's useful. Every phrase corresponds to one of the three dimensions that are your concern as a task manager. "Leadership is a process of creating a vision . . . in accord with the leader's purpose or the shared purpose of all." We believe that this is another way of saying a leader determines what is important. In fact, articulating a vision and mission for an organization is an excellent way of setting the agenda for what is important, your first concern when applying the task management model. An effective leader always works hard at separating the noise from the signal.

"Communicating [the vision], influencing others to carry it out, and setting an example that inspires and directs the actions of others." These activities set the stage for increasing the capability of people and elevating their enjoyment of work. In other words, this part of the definition speaks directly to how you motivate people by assigning tasks thoughtfully and strategically and enabling employees to gain access to the competencies needed to succeed. Assigning and enabling are essential for practicing task management decision making—they are also a big part of leadership success.

Specifically, let's break it down to show how certain task management skills contribute to the leadership definition:

1. A leader *creates a vision.*

Supporting Task Management Activities:

- Determines what the important tasks are that he and his direct reports will focus on.
- Sets a direction and determines priorities.
- Develops a mission as a blueprint for achieving the vision.
- Works toward bottom-line results.

2. A leader *communicates the vision and influences people to carry it out.*

Supporting Task Management Activities:

- Creates and encourages two-way candid communication.
- Holds problem-solving sessions.
- Assigns the right jobs to the right people.

3. A leader *sets an example.*

Supporting Task Management Activities:

- Behaves as the embodiment of what he want others to believe in by
  - Working on appropriate important tasks himself.
  - Not hogging the limelight.
  - Showing discipline with his own big Ds.
  - Walking the talk.
- Assigns and enables employees to do important tasks.
- Stops people from doing below-the-line tasks.

4. A leader *inspires people.*

Supporting Task Management Activities:

- Assigns gold stars.
- Requires big Ds to get done.
- Assigns yellow flags with help and teams.

- Enlists employees to work directly on behalf of the vision, mission, values, and goals of the organization.

5. A leader *directs and focuses people's efforts. Supporting Task Management Activities:*

- Keeps people working above the line.
- Assigns and monitors tasks with deliberation and forethought.
- Counsels and confronts direct reports regarding below-the-line tasks.
- Reevaluates priorities in a timely manner and determines if what was important is still important now.

We began this chapter by reintroducing style in order to recommend the Q4 style as the one that will best equip you to employ the task management model. When you put it all together, you will be doing as a manager what effective leaders do. Like a good leader, you understand that you ultimately will achieve your goals by how skillfully you work with people—developing their capabilities, coaching and counseling, promoting teamwork, building partnerships, guiding, and establishing direction.

Practicing task management is a natural conduit to becoming a good leader. Whoever the designated leaders are in your company, as a task manager, you may find that more and more the role is being filled by you.

LEADERSHIP STYLES AND TASK MANAGEMENT ELEMENTS

	Q1	Q2
CORE BELIEFS	**Can't rely on or trust people; "Just do it!"**	**Can't rely on people Avoids them**
"IMPORTANCE" DIMENSION	Intense interest in short-term results for important tasks	No concern for sorting out important and nonimportant tasks
"CAPABILITY" DIMENSION	Lack of knowledge of capabilities of people Little concern for skill development	Doesn't care about matching skills to tasks Poor development of skills
"ENJOYMENT" DIMENSION	No regard for job satisfaction Doesn't care if people like or dislike tasks	No concern for job satisfaction No empathy
ASSIGNING TASKS	Watches and tells people how to do even gold star tasks Keeps all tasks within function Offers little help on yellow flag or big D tasks Discourages teamwork on yellow flag tasks	Doesn't monitor performance Doesn't know what people are working on Doesn't stop people from working below the line
GETTING THINGS DONE (RESULTS)	Uses fear to make people perform Effort frittered away for short-term results	Mechanically assigns tasks to person closest to him The wrong things get done

LEADERSHIP STYLES AND TASK MANAGEMENT ELEMENTS *(Continued)*

	Q3	Q4
CORE BELIEFS	**Keep people happy with enjoyable work**	**Grow through getting important tasks done**
"IMPORTANCE" DIMENSION	Allows lots of below-the-line activity to avoid conflict or tension More emphasis on raising morale than doing important work	Strives to make all assignments above the line
"CAPABILITY" DIMENSION	Overestimates people's skills Emphasizes who will *enjoy* rather than who is *capable*	Tries to match tasks with competence Uses coaching, skill development, and teamwork to build competency
"ENJOYMENT" DIMENSION	Overemphasis on enjoyment at expense of productivity Seeks path of least resistance to keep everyone happy	Tries to build enjoyment through mastering of skills and a stake in the process
ASSIGNING TASKS	Finds what people like and assigns it to them No distinction between busy work and vital work Has trouble stopping basement activity	Provides help and teamwork for yellow flag tasks Tries to make assignments gold star tasks Provides counseling and monitoring for big Ds Uses constructive confrontation for red flags and below-line activities
GETTING THINGS DONE (RESULTS)	Untimely, mediocre performance	Above-average results achieved on important tasks Little time wasted on nonproductive work

CHAPTER 7

CHECKLIST FOR TOMORROW

To the fearful, [change] . . . is threatening because it means that things might get worse. To the hopeful it is encouraging because things may get better. To the confident it is inspiring because the challenge exists to make things better.

King Whitney, Jr., president,
Personnel Laboratory, Inc.

Your interest in this book indicates that you are ready to consider new ideas as you work toward the goal of getting the right things done—through people. You are willing to think about the reality around you a little differently as a manager and modify your behavior to do a better job.

Actually, the "new" ideas presented here are not new at all for the scores of successful managers and leaders who have been putting them into practice for decades. In this sense, the task management model has already proven itself.

We hope that you will begin using this analytical tool to help reveal why work gets bogged down and to offer remedies for improving bottom-line performance. Remember from Chapter 1 some of the problems that frustrate managers:

- Overseeing a department full of busy people who never seem to get as much accomplished as they should.
- Running around frantically to do a job yourself rather than assigning it when something really important comes up.

- Feeling discouraged about your ability to influence people—you feel unable to jump-start them into action.

Armed with the task management model and what you know about Q4-style behavior, you should now feel that you can get a handle on these kinds of problems.

The nice thing is that you don't have to turn your world upside down to start applying what you have learned. You don't have to call a meeting and announce that everyone's going to be working on more gold stars and no red flags. Your direct reports never have to know the difference between Q1 and Q4 behavior. You can start applying task management and making better-informed decisions one day at a time until scanning your workplace environment in a more analytical way becomes a habit—a winning habit.

Here's a convenient checklist that recaps the major points:

KNOW WHAT IS IMPORTANT

1. **Know your organization's vision, mission, values, and goals.**

2. **Know your organization's strategies and operational plans.**

3. **Know what your boss's goals are.**

4. **Know what your own goals are.** One way to make sure that you know is to ask your boss what the key objectives are that you could accomplish this year.

5. **Review your job description with your boss.**

KNOW WHO IS CAPABLE AMONG YOUR PEOPLE AND WHAT THEY ENJOY DOING

1. Observe your people at work, in meetings, and in one-to-one discussions with them. Take note of their strengths, weaknesses, skills, abilities, interests, preferences, likes, and dislikes.

2. Connect with your people. Hold open-ended discussions in which you probe, inviting them to talk about their background, technical knowledge, education, and previous job experiences. Find out about their interests and preferences and what they feel their strongest competencies and weaknesses are. It's amazing what people will tell you if you ask!

3. If your company provides testing, study each person's test results. You can learn quite a lot about their cognitive skills, intellect, drive, and character from professionally administered tests.

4. If you have access to previous performance reviews of your people, read them and note their strengths and weaknesses. This includes talking to others (prior bosses, peers, direct reports) to learn as much as possible about each person.

5. Manage by walking around with a purpose. Observe and study your people in action.

6. Be very conscientious and analytical in completing performance reviews of your people. It's surprising how much you can uncover about their capabilities by thinking in depth about your direct reports. For example, how do they go about tackling problems and issues? How conceptual and strategic are they? How are their verbal (written and oral) skills? Can they think quantitatively? Can they sort through and identify key issues from an array of information? What seems to attract them and capture their thinking? When are they disinterested?

7. **If 360-degree feedback appraisals are available, use information from these reports to help you determine strengths and weaknesses.** This is a great way to learn how key people, such as direct reports, peers, vendors, and even customers, perceive this person.

Even with all this information, a manager must still add her own judgment in determining what is important, who is capable, and if he or she will enjoy an assignment. This is the intuitive or subjective side of managing effectively.

You will always have to make judgment calls and hope that you have reached the best decisions. However, the quality of your decisions will be buttressed by the objective data you gather. Weighing the three components of importance, capability, and enjoyment and then making an informed assignment will determine to a large degree your success as a leader.

PRESCRIPTIONS

Here is a summary of the prescriptions that have been made along the way based on your ongoing assessment of the components of the task management model:

1. *If you assign a gold star:*

- Let that person alone. He doesn't need help except to know that it's his responsibility.
- Monitor progress at jointly agreed checkpoints.
- Give him lots of freedom and watch his enthusiasm catch fire.
- In short, give him *directed autonomy,* the freedom to approach the task in his own way, but with direction and oversight.

2. *If you assign a big D:*

- Don't just assign it and walk away.
- Conduct an in-depth discussion and allow the person to vent or talk through her misgivings. Listen at a thinking level without being judgmental.
- Don't back down from the assignment without good reason.
- State the benefits to her, to the organization, and to you if it gets done.
- Stress the urgency of getting it done, and assign a specific timeline and date for achieving it.
- Build in checkpoints along the way to monitor progress. Be assertive in holding these touch-base sessions.
- Keep repeating the benefits as she progresses.

- If procrastination occurs, confront it and talk it through.
- As she reaches milestones in achieving the task, be generous with praise to reward her, that is, pay her some "psychological income."
- If necessary, turn up the thermostat of pressure.

3. *If you assign a yellow flag:*

- Provide access to the complementary skills he will need to complete the task.
- Talk through who will be helping him, the skills or competencies they will bring to the task, and the importance of approaching this task with a team effort.
- Because the task is important and he likes it, he may feel strongly that he can do it alone. Don't let his enthusiasm for the assignment override your judgment that he will need help to get it done.
- If he recommends people to help him, talk through his assessment of their strengths and weaknesses to ensure that he is putting together a group of people with the necessary complementary skills and not just friends who are "nice to work with."
- Make sure that he understands that he is the one who is responsible and accountable for

getting it done—not the group. In other words, he is the team leader.

- Clearly articulate the benefits of achieving this task—notably how it could help him develop new skills and competencies. Also highlight the benefits to him, to the organization, and to you if it is achieved.
- Set up touch-base sessions for progress review that are maintained vigorously.
- Ask him to establish with his team a plan and goals for achieving this assignment with an understanding that he personally will review progress.
- If this is the first time he has ever led a group, counsel him on team skills.
- Limit the number of yellow flags.

4. *If you have assigned a red flag:*

- Reassign it immediately to someone else for whom it would be a gold star, big D, or yellow flag.
- Counsel the person, explaining your reasons for making the reassignment. Be sure that her self-esteem is not adversely affected by the change. (It builds self-esteem to assign something important to do. So taking it away may make her feel threatened, even if she is incapable of doing it or wouldn't enjoy it.)

5. *Stop people from working on black hole activities:*

- Reassign employees to gold stars, big Ds, or yellow flags. Get them working upstairs as much as possible.
- Don't be seduced by people working in black holes who enjoy the task. Because they derive pleasure and satisfaction from doing something well, they will offer you abundant reasons why the task is important. For example, they often will say that it has long-term value or that it is an experimental idea.
- Don't let people work in the basement just to keep them busy.

6. *Think through what you could really accomplish by assigning more and more gold stars:*

- More gold star assignments will allow you to achieve goals with greater speed, accuracy, and quality. The organization comes alive when the number of gold star assignments increases.
- Cultivate methods for developing and training people so that they are more likely to be assigned gold star tasks. One way is to make sure that they are on teams that are engaged in yellow flag activities. Thus they will learn through experience. Also, training and development programs, cross-functional assignments, task force assignments, and attendance

at problem-solving meetings all can help people build skills and competencies. This sets the stage for increasing gold stars.

OTHER RECOMMENDATIONS

1. Don't let the enjoyment component (pleasure principle) stand in the way of making an assignment. Some managers allow this to dominate their thinking when assigning tasks. Although important, don't obsess over how enjoyable the task will be. With sound coaching and follow-up, a direct report may take a seemingly unenjoyable big D and turn it into a gold star. Mature leaders realize that the higher they rise in their organization, the more big Ds they have to do themselves or to delegate, but if too much time is spent concerned about the enjoyment factor, this in itself becomes a basement activity.

2. Don't let the organization chart be a barrier to making an assignment. We've made the point emphatically in other chapters that if you allow vital work to be put into the wrong hands from blind devotion to the organization chart, you could be turning a gold star into a red or yellow flag.

It is sad to say, but reliance on assigning work according to a fixed hierarchy can become ingrained as part of a company's culture. However, this doesn't have to be. In a *Harvard Business Review* article, Charles Knight, chairman of Emerson, arguably one of the best-managed companies in the country, stated, "To keep people motivated and involved, we've tried to avoid problems that can paralyze corporations—things like organization charts. . . . We don't have a published corporate organization chart at Emerson. No such piece of paper exists because we want people to communicate around plans, projects, and problems, not along organizational lines."*

3. Don't think that the most important part of your job as a manager is to determine what is important. Some managers and leaders spend most of their time developing visions, missions, values, plans, and goals but devote little time to working these through the organization and implementing them quickly and effectively. They don't devote enough time to getting this activity assigned to the right people or enabling the people chosen to do it. You need to maintain a balance between thinking through not only what's important but also how it is going to be executed.

4. Don't simply assign people important tasks and walk away from them as if to say, "There! I have delegated! It's up to them to get it done. I'm practicing good hands-off management." The only time you can walk away is when you know an assignment is a gold star. Even then, you need to monitor and review. *Enabling* means to "make one able to do something." Making one able to accomplish something is thought-

*Charles F. Knight, "Emerson Electric: Consistent Profits, Consistently." *Harvard Business Review* (January–February 1992):68.

ful empowerment. Thus, for a big D, yellow flag, or red flag task, you must follow up.

5. Remember that what's important can change quickly. What is important today can be unimportant tomorrow. The vice chairman of a retail department store chain says that the first thing he does every morning is reassess his priorities to determine if he and his people are really working on what is vital. What was upstairs work yesterday could be in the basement today.

6. Don't allow people to turn important tasks into black holes. The pleasure principle can play tricks on our thinking. A direct report can take an assignment he doesn't enjoy and isn't capable of doing and modify it to become a task that is irrelevant—but now he loves it and does it well. This problem is most likely to occur when your communication isn't specific. If you are ambiguous, a direct report might even twist a big D into a black hole. This is one way to turn a job into a hobby.

In our final chapter we will look at how the model can help you with the work that *you* do.

CHAPTER 8

WORKING IN FRONT OF A MIRROR

What we must decide is perhaps how we are valuable, rather than how valuable we are.

F. Scott Fitzgerald,
American author

The famous publisher William Randolph Hearst reportedly once offered Arthur Brisbane, one of his prized newspaper columnists, the opportunity to take a 6-month rest with all expenses paid as a reward for the fine work he had done.

Brisbane turned down the offer, saying, "First of all, I'm afraid that if I quit for 6 months, the circulation of your newspapers may go down. Secondly, I'm afraid that it may not."

It's always difficult to be objective—to know where you stand and exactly what your worth is to your organization. This book has tried to improve your potential contribution by asking you to do some honest soul searching about how you think as a manager assigning work.

Let's assume that over time you apply the principles of task management consistently to the decisions you make about your employees. You find that your people are working more proficiently on tasks that really contribute to the goals you've developed. However, to get the most from task management, you will still need to make sure that one other person in your organization is getting the right things done. You!

Task management is a powerful tool for bringing out the best in others. You can apply that same tool to make sure that *your own* contributions are meaningful and to challenge yourself to get the most from the work you do. How do you spend your time? Will you use the three dimensions of importance, capability, and enjoyment when deciding what tasks *you* will do? In other words, are you prepared to look in the mirror and ask the same questions with respect to yourself that you're asking as you assign work?

As we said earlier, our starting point assumes that you have qualified people in the appropriate job positions. Even so, your direct reports have unique strengths and weaknesses. You now realize how critical it is to take these into account whenever you make an assignment. Likewise, we assume that you are the right person to be doing your job. If you turn the spotlight on yourself, you see that you also have strengths and weaknesses. You have a unique combination of talents, capabilities, skills, and yes, deficiencies and shortcomings. In fact, the farther you advance in your organization, the more gaps you almost certainly will have in knowledge and competencies in areas over which you have responsibility.

Why is this? Traditionally, each time you are promoted, you manage either different segments or oversee a larger part of the entire organization. This goes beyond your original expertise. Thus the cost accountant becomes the head of her department. She may become the CFO some day, in which case her duties will far exceed the knowledge and capabilities of a cost accountant. Eventually, if she becomes, say, president of the company, she will be required to know a lot about every area of her organization.

Obviously, her ability to go that far requires that along the way she learn many new skills and a tremendous amount of information in order to be effective. In terms of the task management model, this kind of growth and advancement means tackling yellow flags and finding ways to fill those gaps. As you can see, though, the gaps don't become smaller with increased responsibility. They grow larger.

It's important, then, to monitor closely the way you spend your time. How would you assess yourself as you look in the mirror both in terms of (1) the tasks that confront you as part of your management responsibilities and (2) all the other tasks that make up the obligations of your job?

THE TASK OF MANAGING YOURSELF

The following informal questionnaire will help you to take a thoughtful look at your own performance in terms of task management. Be completely honest in order to get an accurate and helpful picture of how you approach your work and your own tasks:

- Are you anxious to get to work every day, eager to start?
- Are you energized by your job, or does it wear you down and sap your strength?

- Do you understand your boss's goals?
- Do you fully understand what is expected of you and how you will be evaluated?
- Do you know when you are succeeding and when you are missing the mark?
- Do you spend time working on black holes?
- Do you find yourself doing red flags?
- Are you working on any yellow flags that challenge you to grow in your capabilities and advance in your organization?
- If so, are you willing to get appropriate help to be successful with the yellow flags?
- Do you work on enough gold stars to help make your job rewarding and satisfying?
- On the other hand, do you keep too many gold stars for yourself that others could do perhaps even better than you?

We can't speak for what you want to gain from your job or from life for that matter. An assumption of this book is that you are a capable person who wants to get more of the right things done. If you could do that, we assume, not only would you be more successful in your current job and career, but you also would gain a great deal of personal satisfaction and growth as well.

As you keep in mind how you answered the preceding questions, let's take another look at how you handle the three dimensions of the task management model *from the perspective of how you handle your own assignments.*

BLACK HOLES

The first step in eliminating them is to admit that you have some black holes in your working life. Most of us do because it's human nature. Although unnecessary, we usually enjoy black hole activity and allow ourselves to be seduced into thinking that we are spending time on something meaningful even if it has no value to the company. Worse, sometimes managers even know full well that their black holes are worthless but keep doing them anyway as guilty pleasures. They may rationalize that a black hole makes up for all the grief they put up with the rest of the time.

As you advance in your career, you may be more susceptible to indulging in black hole activity simply because you will become more autonomous and may be questioned less about how you spend your time.

The only remedy, of course, is for you to examine your time and confront yourself about working on what is unimportant. Do you spend time with this vendor or that seller because you actually might be doing business together or just because it's enjoyable? Do you have a pet project that has long ago proven itself irrelevant and going nowhere, yet you hate to give it up or the time you put into it? Are there certain rituals or procedures that are totally unproductive but you follow anyway out of habit?

In certain cases only you can judge if a task is a black hole. No one else may even realize it. But such black holes are robbing you and your company of your time and energy. If you look fondly at enjoyable black holes as a change of pace, an enjoyable break, or an alternative to stress in your job, consider replacing them with gold stars. Then you can do something enjoyable and have the satisfaction of knowing that you aren't spending your time in the basement.

Another very important reason for avoiding black holes is the message it sends to everyone around you. If you spend time on the job in black hole territory, it will give some employees an excuse to do it themselves. This is another area where you have to walk the talk. No matter how important you say it is to avoid working in the basement, if people see you doing it, they will have a hard time believing you.

RED FLAGS

While black holes should not be assigned to you or anyone else, red flags need to be assigned to someone because they are important tasks. However, that someone should *not* be you. In fact, what is a red flag for you would be someone else's yellow flag, big D, or even gold star if it were assigned correctly.

So the same logic should apply to you as it does when you are making assignments for your direct reports. The chances of your doing a red flag task successfully are very poor. If you give yourself a red flag or you are assigned one by your boss, you should work to have it reassigned. You might recommend a better person to do it based on your task management analysis.

If this is not possible, you may have to try to accomplish that task. However, if red flags are being assigned to you frequently, it not only hurts your productivity and morale, but it also hurts what your organization is trying to accomplish. Work to change or enlighten so that you don't have red flags on your plate.

BIG Ds

Once again, it's human nature to put off and avoid handling our own big Ds. Understand, though, that by definition if they are *your* big Ds, only *you* can deal with them. Passing them off to become someone else's big Ds is not a fair solution and will create ill will. The only remedy is to be your own stern taskmaster for getting them done.

We recognize that this is an additional burden for you the more you function as a leader. As we said, because of their level of authority, company leaders are often the only ones who can do some of the most thankless and disagreeable tasks, such as reducing head count, cutting the budget, and reallocating resources. So it doesn't get any easier. As you advance in your career, the buck may stop at your desk more frequently.

Further, the more authority you have, the less likely it is that you will be called to task if you procrastinate about big Ds. This means that you may only have the mirror to face as you deal with big Ds.

Will you put off a difficult but important task or confront it and do what has to be done sooner rather than later?

By the way, in their own way, everyday big Ds can be a problem for an organization as much as more dramatic tasks. Returning telephone calls, e-mails, or any other communication is important. While these "chores" can feel like a millstone around your neck, *not* doing them in a timely way can be costly to your company. If information is the lifeblood of an organization, letting these big Ds pile up is a blockage in the arteries. The same is true for turning reports in late, procrastinating on performance reviews, and neglecting to give feedback in a timely way. Mundane? Perhaps, but these big Ds *must* get done!

YELLOW FLAGS

You know by now that a yellow flag can be an opportunity to learn and grow in your job. Completing yellow flag tasks successfully can expand your worth to your company and open up new career paths—that is, if you are willing to take on yellow flags and acknowledge that you need assistance in becoming competent in a new endeavor.

Too often people in leadership and management roles feel that showing a need for training, coaching, or other assistance is a weakness. They don't want to be seen as coming up short in any area of their organization. They think that they will look bad in front of their bosses, and in some corporate cultures, they may be right. Therefore, they don't venture out of the job slot they are in or the routine they've created for themselves. They may never increase their skills unless someone pushes them to do so. They may never take on a challenge unless someone makes them.

You should view a gap in your skills or knowledge as an opportunity and not a flaw. Just as you would welcome a direct report who seeks help in gaining competency to take on a yellow flag, you should have the same attitude about those yellow flags that are opportunities for you to grow. You have to challenge yourself, though, because you may be in the position simply to assign them to someone else and pass up your opportunity.

You also have to allow yourself the time to get up to speed. You may have to pursue formal education, training, or tutoring. It may require finding a mentor or teaming with someone who is competent in your area of need. However you go about gaining what you need, you must see the short-term interruption as worthwhile.

GOLD STARS

It shouldn't take much effort to convince you that you should have some gold stars. We all need them. So don't give them all away. If you are the best person to accomplish a gold star task, keep it. Your enthusiasm for your job will be influenced greatly by the gold stars in your life. They help to offset the big Ds you must deal with. Gold stars let you do something for your company, but they do something for you as well.

The only caution, which we've stated before, is that you not hoard all the gold stars for yourself. It won't take long for your direct reports to catch on if you are always ready to intercept a gold star and deprive them of experiencing the satisfaction of doing meaningful work that is enjoyable. Eventually, some may resent it enough to leave. Others might not express their disappointment, but it's safe to say their motivation and commitment may never be full scale if you keep all the gold stars.

It is particularly disappointing to them if they are better equipped to complete a gold star task than you are. And this is an important test, along with timing, availability, and so on. If a manager keeps a gold star that she can't do at least as well as or better than her direct reports, she doesn't just rob that person of a fulfilling experience, but she also keeps her company from getting the most from that assignment.

A TASK ANALYSIS GUIDE

To help you to decide if a task is right for you and if it is a black hole, red flag, big D, yellow flag, or gold star, we have provided copies of a simple task analysis form on the following pages. It rates a task using elements of the task management model. It is self-explanatory, and if you are completely honest in your rating, you will get a better idea of how to assign that task. Of course, this form also can be used for tasks you assign to your employees.

TASK ANALYSIS

TASK____

IMPACT ON BUSINESS______________________________

____

UNIMPORTANT	1	2	3	4	5	IMPORTANT
INCAPABLE	1	2	3	4	5	CAPABLE
DESPISE	1	2	3	4	5	ENJOY
NOT NEED HELP	1	2	3	4	5	NEED HELP

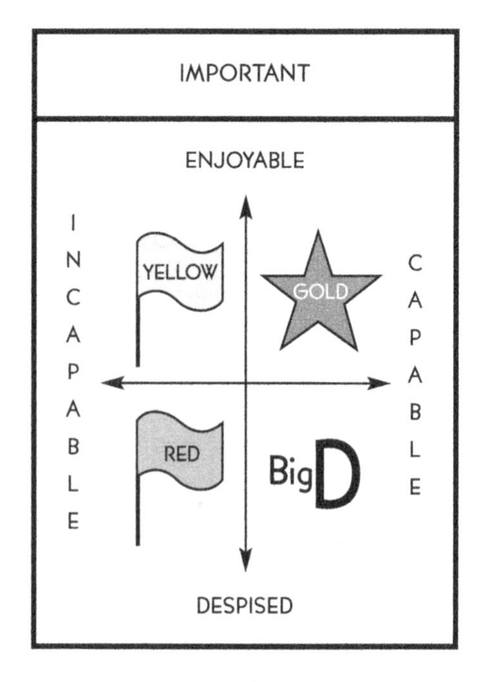

TASK ANALYSIS

TASK____

IMPACT ON BUSINESS____________________________

____

UNIMPORTANT	1	2	3	4	5	IMPORTANT
INCAPABLE	1	2	3	4	5	CAPABLE
DESPISE	1	2	3	4	5	ENJOY
NOT NEED HELP	1	2	3	4	5	NEED HELP

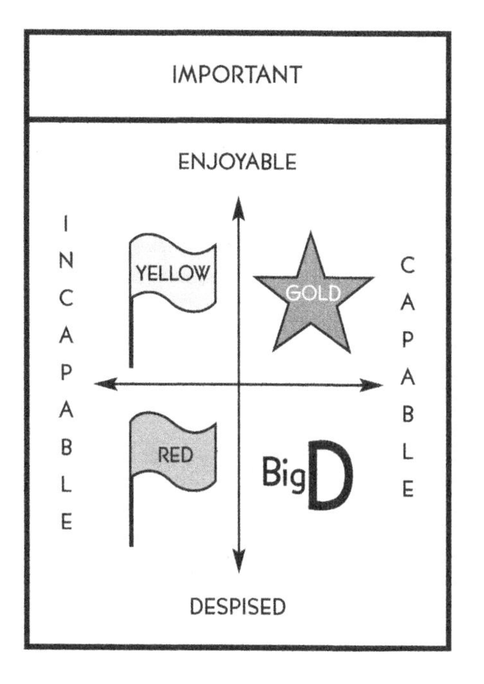

TASK ANALYSIS

TASK____

IMPACT ON BUSINESS____________________________

____

UNIMPORTANT	1	2	3	4	5	IMPORTANT
INCAPABLE	1	2	3	4	5	CAPABLE
DESPISE	1	2	3	4	5	ENJOY
NOT NEED HELP	1	2	3	4	5	NEED HELP

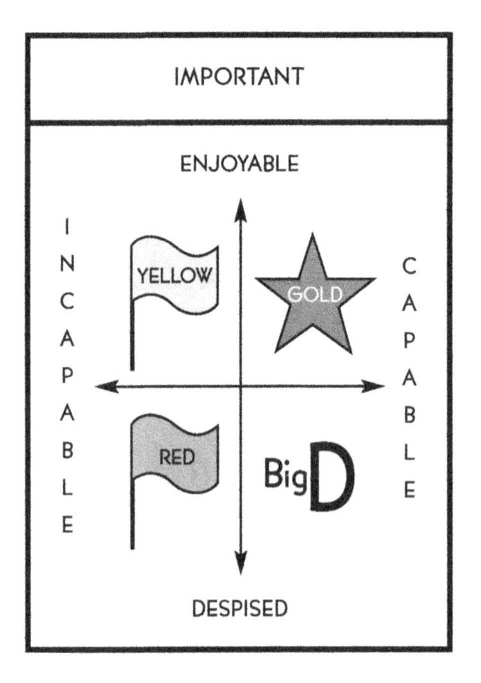

DEVELOP YOUR SKILLS AT THE *GETTING THINGS DONE WORKSHOP*

If you want additional motivation and reinforcement for putting into practice the task management concepts explained in this book, you can attend a workshop designed exclusively around *Why Can't We Get Anything Done Around Here?*

The *Getting Things Done Workshop* offers the opportunity to work with the ideas and principles you've read about so that you can apply them directly to your own work situation. In fact, you also may want colleagues and staff members to participate to help them become more productive, too.

Offered in one-day or half-day versions, the workshop uses interactive techniques to solidify understanding of the book's ideas and principles. This means that hands-on activities and experience-based learning will replace traditional lectures to provide a lively learning environment.

The workshop will help you to develop the habit of applying the book's system on the job, offering practice in determining the most productive way to handle every work assignment you make.

You can schedule a *Getting Things Done Workshop* to be held exclusively for your organization either on site or at a convenient nearby meeting facility.

To make arrangements or to learn more about the *Getting Things Done Workshop*, contact the workshop sponsor, Psychological Associates, 8112 Maryland Avenue, Suite 300, St. Louis, MO 63105, 1-866-258-0369, *info@q4solutions.com* or visit *www.q4solutions.com* for more information.

INDEX

ABOUT THE AUTHORS

Robert E. Lefton is cofounder, president, and CEO of Psychological Associates, a leading U.S. management and organizational consultancy servicing many Fortune 500 companies. He presently serves on numerous business boards and has been an advisor to CEOs and boards of directors in such areas as executive succession, performance reviews for senior executives, strategic planning, organizational change, and teams.

Jerome T. Loeb is former chairman of The Mays Department Stores Company. He retired in 2001 after a 37-year career with May Company and at which time May Company had just completed its twenty-seventh consecutive year of increased sales and earnings per share. Mr. Loeb is currently adjunct professor of marketing at the Olin School of Business, Washington University in St. Louis.